weebee Series Two (Books 9 – 16) Complete Resource Book

✝ CROSSBRIDGE BOOKS

Published by:
Crossbridge Books
Worcester

© R M Price-Mohr 2021

All rights reserved. No part of this publication may be reproduced, stored in a retrieval system or transmitted in any form or by any means – electronic, mechanical, recording or otherwise – without prior permission of the copyright owner.

Permission is given to photocopy the resource pages.

ISBN 978-1-913946-36-4

weebee Series Two Resource Book (Books 9 – 16)

This book contains photocopy-able pages with games and activities designed to support the learning of vocabulary and targeted phonic sounds used in weebee series two (Books 9 – 16). A list of the new vocabulary introduced with each book along with the story text is provided for all books. Lists of the target phonic sounds and high frequency words are also included for each book. The phonic sounds largely follow the 'Letters and Sounds' phonic phases. The high frequency words are from the 100 most common words in written English that comprise, on average, one half of all reading materials. A handbook and other resources can be downloaded free of charge from the website: https://crossbridgeeducational.com

Instructions for Series Two Games

Books 9 to 12 have three games: Grog's Journey, snakes and ladders, and Pento.

The boards are made of four sheets that can be laminated and taped together.

Grog's Journey requires each player to have a counter. Players take turns to roll a die and the winner is the first to reach the end. Players are encouraged to say the words they land on as they play.

'Snakes and ladders' requires each player to have a counter and follows traditional rules (up a ladder and down a snake). The winner is the first player to reach the end.

Pento requires four players. Each player needs a counter and chooses one of the four weebee characters shown on the board. Using a die, players move around the board in a clockwise direction and if they land on their chosen weebee, they can collect the word card that corresponds to where they have landed. There are five cards for each weebee. The winner is the first to collect all five. If a player lands on one of the four corner colours, they should pick up the matching coloured card from the centre of the board and follow the instructions. If they land on a word that they need they may collect.

Books 13 to 16 have two games: Spectro and HexConnex

Spectro is for 2 – 4 players. Each player needs a counter and a circular lotto board. They each choose a colour to start on. Players move around the large circular board in a clockwise direction. Whatever colour they land on, they take a corresponding card from the centre of the board. If the word is on their board they place it on. If they do not have it (or already have it), it is put back on the bottom of the pile. The winner is the first to fill their board.

HexConnex is for 2 players. Each player needs a board. The green hexagons are spread out so that all the words are visible. Players take turns using the spinner and follow the instructions. The winner is the first to complete a continuous line from left to right. Players should decide before they begin if instructions are compulsory or optional and if they apply to both players' boards or just their own.

weebee Series Two (Books 9-16) Complete Resource Book

Contents: Page

Book 9 (The egg) Word list, targeted phonics, high frequency words and text	4
Grog's Journey	6
Snakes and ladders	14
Pento	22
Phonics sheet (_ee_)	38
Book 10 (The caterpillar) Word list, targeted phonics, high frequency words and text	40
Grog's Journey	42
Snakes and ladders	50
Pento	58
Phonics sheet (_ll)	70
Book 11 (The robot) word list, targeted phonics, high frequency words and text	72
Grog's Journey	74
Snakes and ladders	82
Pento	90
Phonics sheet (_oo_)	102
Book 12 (The robin) word list, targeted phonics, high frequency words and text	104
Grog's Journey	106
Snakes and ladders	114
Pento	122
Phonics sheet (_ow_)	134
Book 13 (The dragon) word list, targeted phonics, high frequency words and text	136
Spectro Board	138
Spectro	146
Hex Connex	162
Hex Connex spinner	168
Phonics sheet (_y)	170
Book 14 (The frog) word list, targeted phonics, high frequency words and text	172
Spectro	174
Hex Connex	190
Phonics sheet (bl_)	196
Book 15 (The troll) word list, targeted phonics, high frequency words and text	198
Spectro	200
Hex Connex	216
Phonics sheet (ch_)	222
Book 16 (The butterfly) word list, targeted phonics, high frequency words and text	224
Spectro	226
Hex Connex	242
Phonics sheet (st_)	248
Pupil Tracking Sheet	250

The egg 9

Word list:

Sun	hot	him	are	cool
Egg	smooth	spots	crack	getting
Bigger	dragon	playing	did	call
Into	ant	spider	wooden	dry

Targeted phonics:

_oo_
_gg
dr_
_nt
sp_

High frequency words:

big
into
him
are
did
get
call

Text:
1. There is a yellow sun in the sky.
2. Grog is very hot. Pip is with him. She is hot as well.
3. They are going to the pond to cool down.
4. Grog can see an egg in the long green grass. Pip can see it as well. The egg is small and smooth. It has red spots.
5. Grog can see a crack in the egg. The crack is getting bigger.
6. This is not a weebee. It is a red dragon. It has green spots. It is very small.
7. The dragon can swim. They are all going to play in the pond.
8. Flup can see them playing in the pond. He will fly down to see them.
9. The egg did not have a nest. The weebees will look for a small nest for the dragon.
10. Flup will call for Tod. Tod can help look for a nest.
11. They go into the tree.
12. They go down into the deep dark roots.
13. They see a bug with black spots. They see a brown ant with red spots. They see a spider with blue spots.
14. Tod can see a nest for the dragon. It is an old wooden box.
15. The dragon can stay with Grog. It is cool and dry in the old tree.

Book 9 Upper left section of Grog's Journey

Book 9 Upper right section of Grog's Journey

Book 9 Lower left section of Grog's Journey

Book 9 Lower right section of Grog's Journey

Book 9 Lower left section of Snakes and Ladders

Book 9 Lower right section of Snakes and Ladders

Book 9 Upper left section of Snakes and Ladders

Book 9 Upper right section of Snakes and Ladders

Book 9 Lower right section of Pento

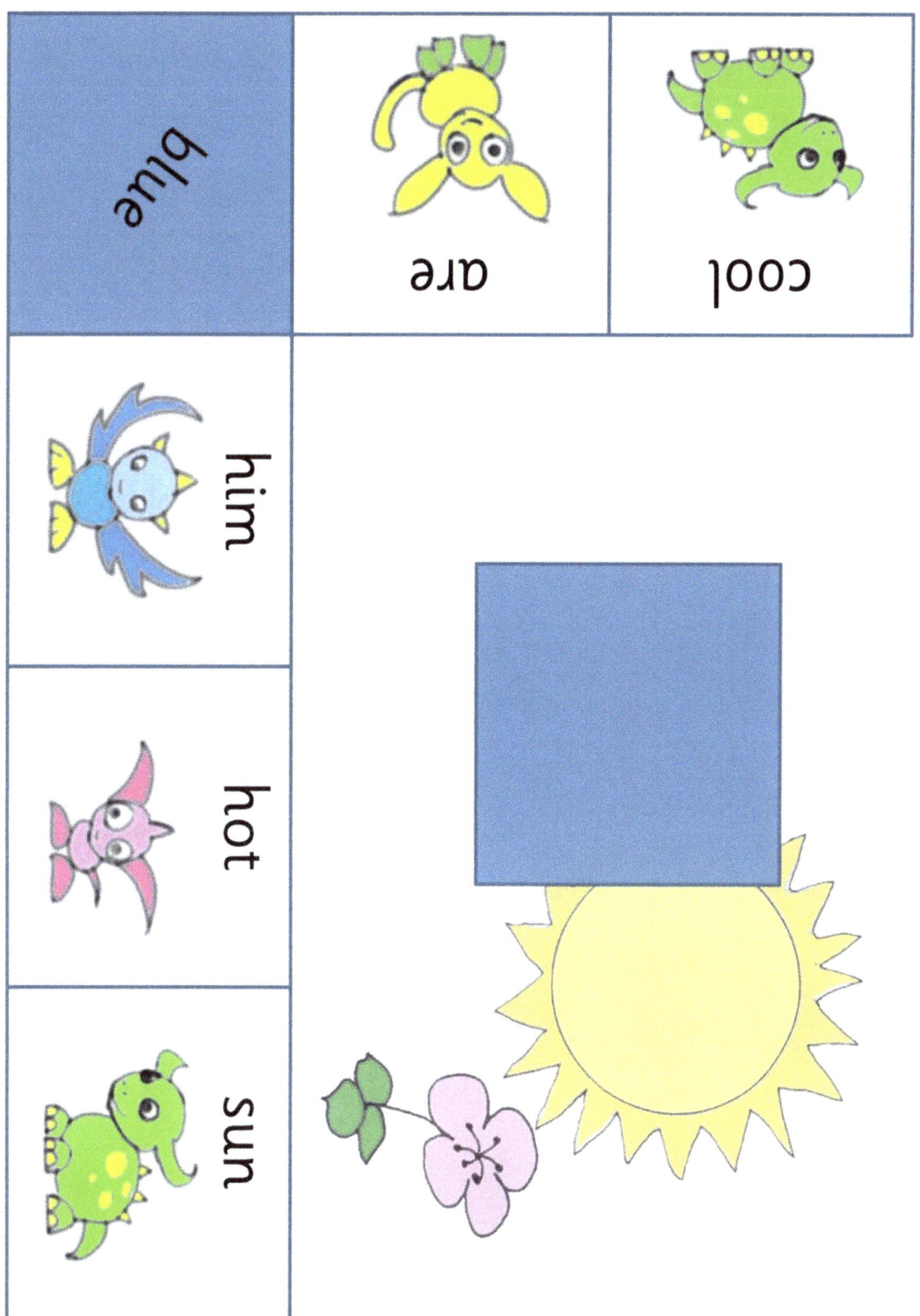

Book 9 Lower left section of Pento

Book 9 Upper right section of Pento

Book 9 Upper left section of Pento

Book 9 Word cards sheet 1 for Pento

Book 9 Word cards sheet 2 for Pento

Go forward one word 1	Go forward two words 2
Go forward three words 3	Go forward four words 4
Go forward five words 5	Go forward six words 6
Go forward one word 1	Go forward two words 2
Go forward three words 3	Go forward four words 4
Go forward five words 5	Go forward six words 6

Book 9 Pink and blue direction cards for Pento (these can be used for books 9 to 12)

Go backward one word 1	Go backward two words 2
Go backward three words 3	Go backward four words 4
Go backward five words 5	Go backward six words 6
Go backward one word 1	Go backward two words 2
Go backward three words 3	Go backward four words 4
Go backward five words 5	Go backward six words 6

Book 9 Yellow and green direction cards for Pento (these can be used for books 9 to 12)

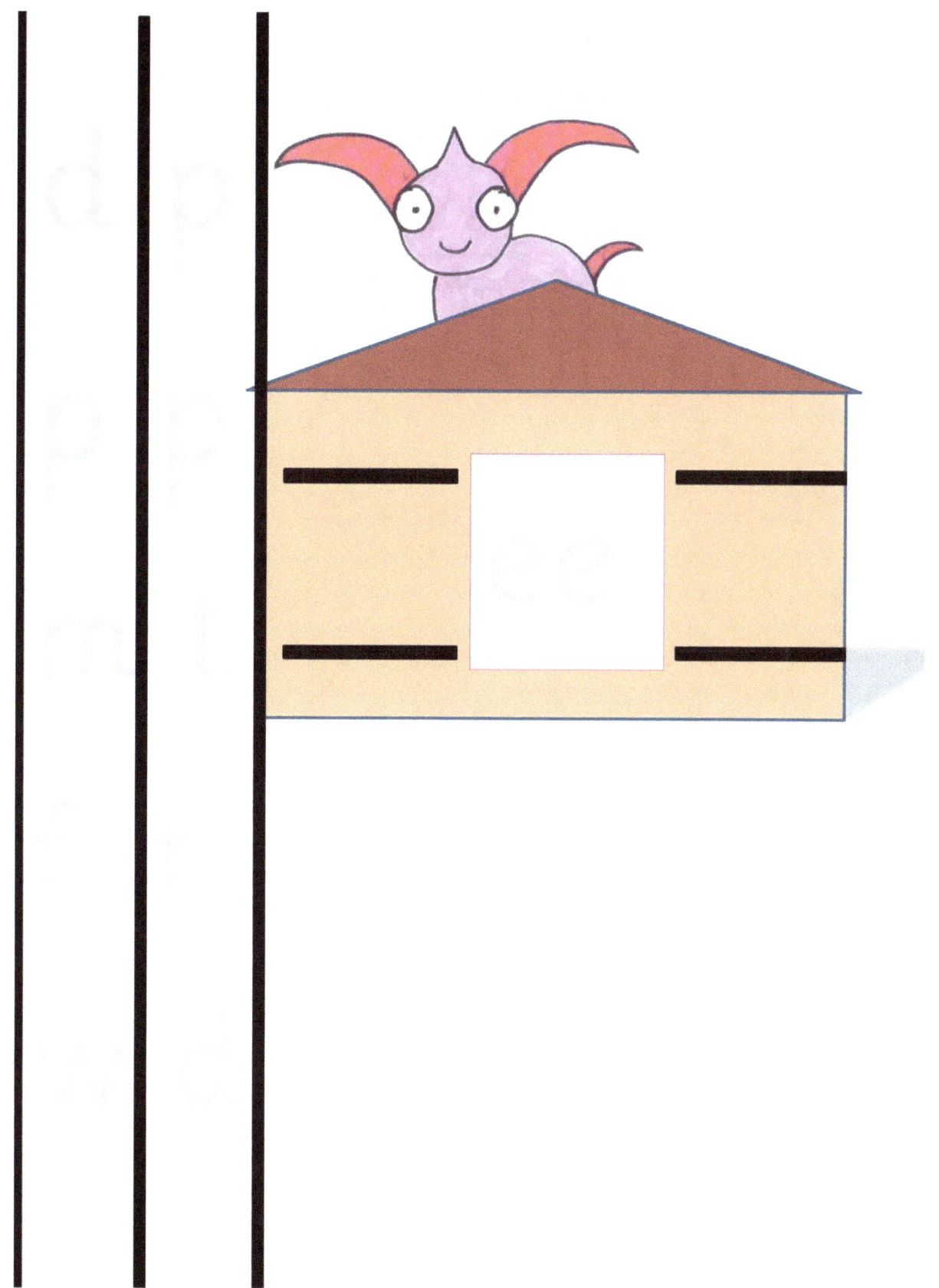

Cut along bold lines and feed through the window

The Caterpillar 10

Word list:

caterpillar	chat	chick	chip	coat
eyes	fluffy	goes	just	little
looking	monster	need	orange	sad
tells	that	meet	two	when

Targeted phonics:

ch_
_oa_
_ee_
_ll_

High frequency words:

look
that
go
just
two
little
when

Text:

1. Zon is going to chat to Tod in the wood.
2. Tod has a smooth chip of wood to put in his nest.
3. Zon is going to get a chip of wood to sit on in his nest.
4. Zon is going back to his shell to see if the wood chip is good to sit on.
5. Now Zon can see his shell. But he is upset. There is a monster in his shell.
6. Zon is going to tell Grog that there is a monster in his shell.
7. Grog and Jig are by the duck. She has a little chick. The chick is yellow and fluffy.
8. Zon tells Grog that there is a monster in his shell. Grog can see that Zon is upset.
9. Grog and Jig go with Zon to see the monster. The fluffy chick is sad to see them go.
10. When they get to the shell they see two big eyes. Now Jig is upset as well.
11. Grog is not upset. He tells Zon and Jig that it is just a caterpillar. It is looking for a nest.
12. The caterpillar is too big for the shell. It will need a bigger nest.
13. Flup can see the caterpillar. He tells the caterpillar to nest in his fluffy hat. But the caterpillar can not fly.
14. The caterpillar goes up the stick. He goes under the old orange coat. Now the caterpillar has a nest and Zon is not upset.

Book 10 Lower left section of Grog's Journey

Book 10 Lower right section of Grog's Journey

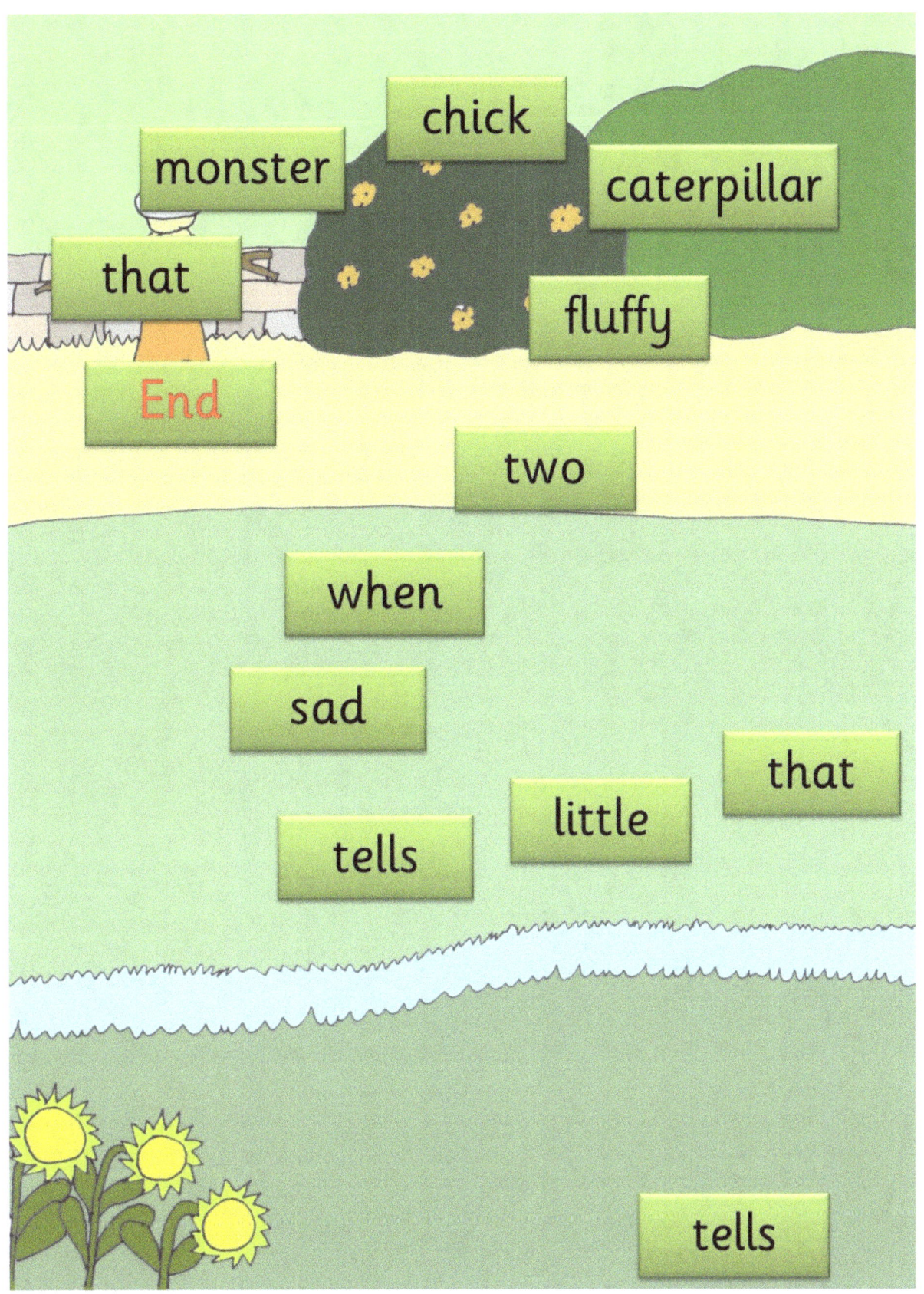

Book 10 Upper left section of Grog's Journey

Book 10 Upper right section of Grog's Journey

Book 10 Lower left section for Snakes and Ladders

Book 10 Lower right section for Snakes and Ladders

Book 10 Upper left section for Snakes and Ladders

Book 10 Upper right section for Snakes and Ladders

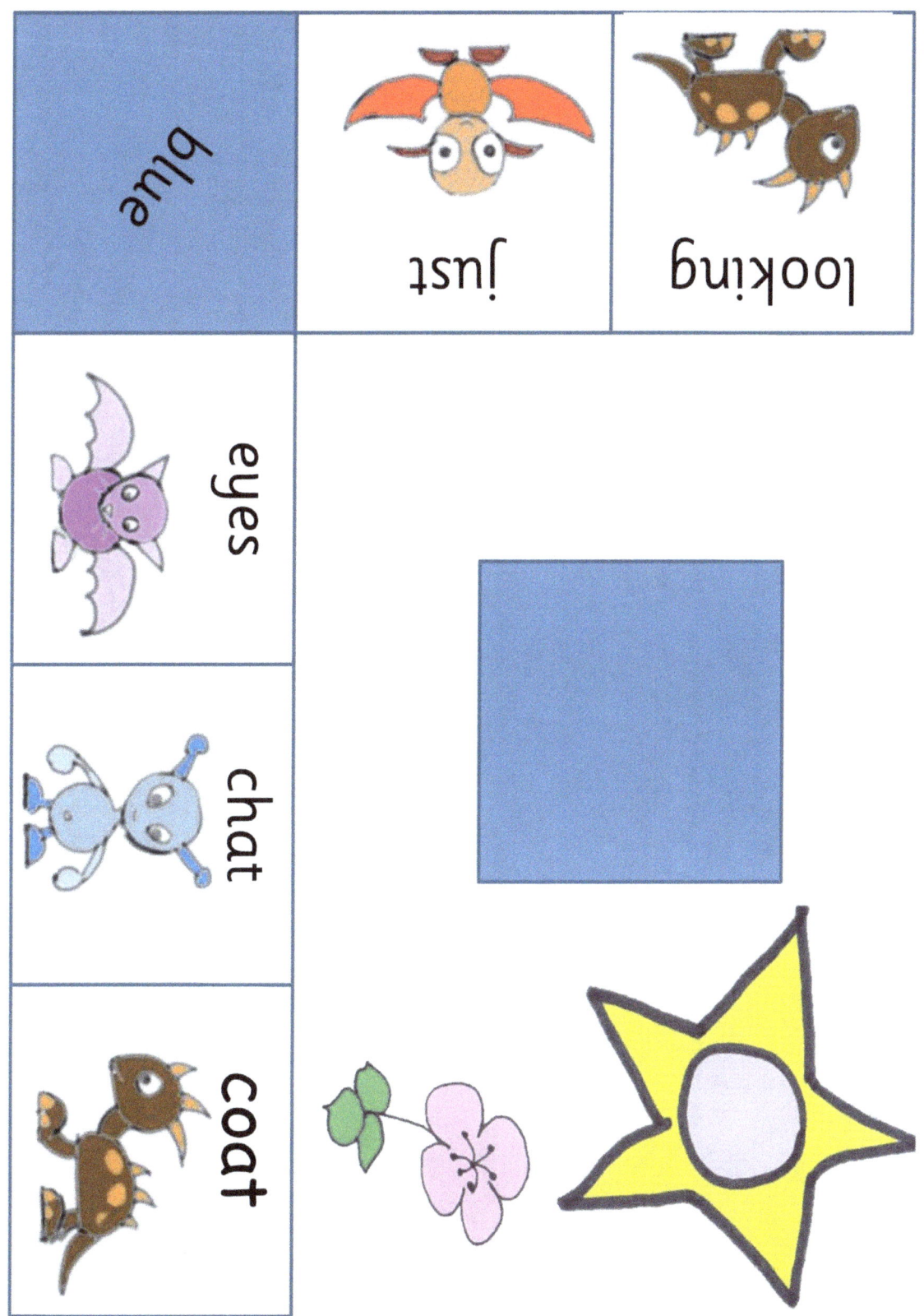

Book 10 Lower left section of Pento

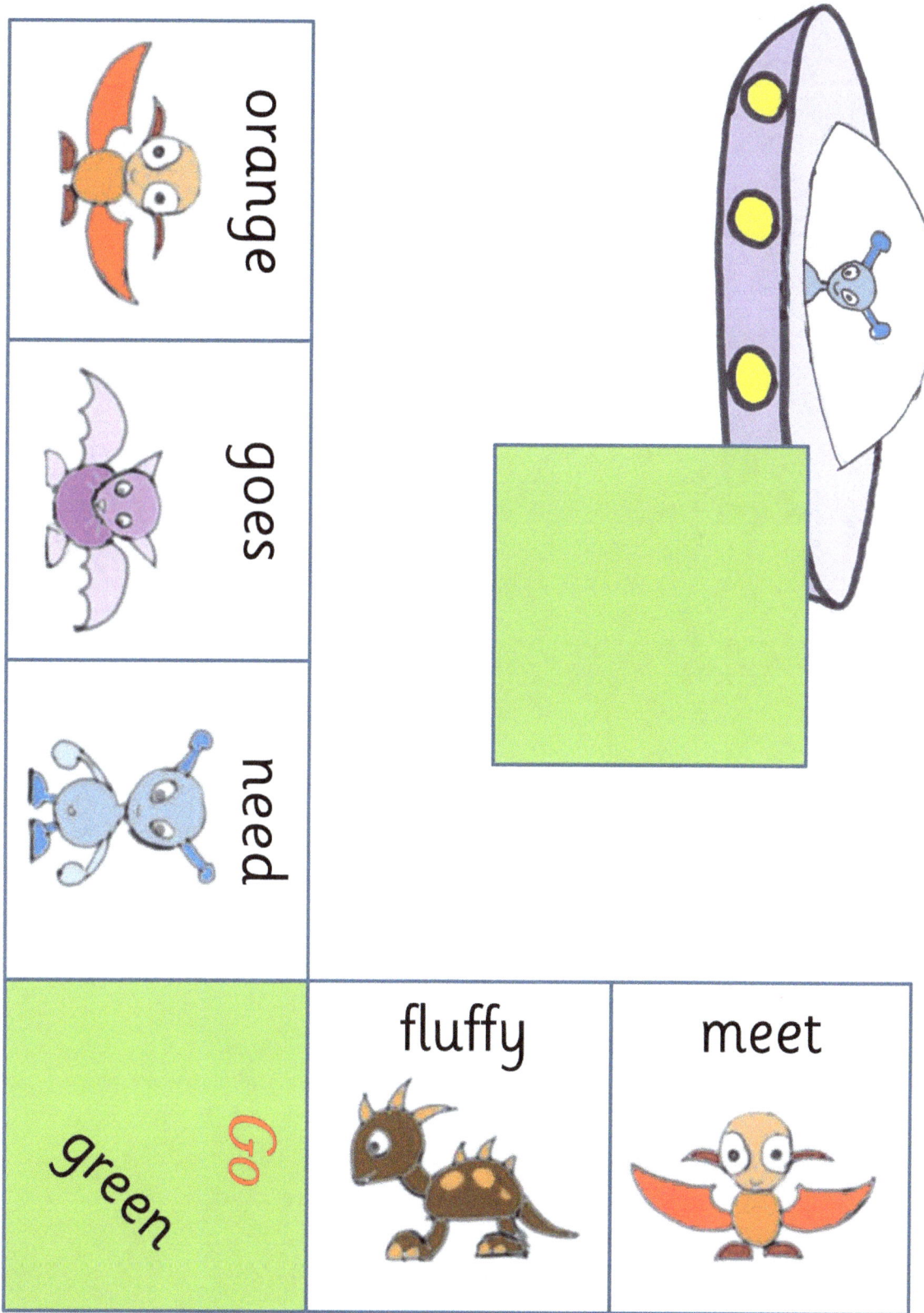

Book 10 Lower right section of Pento

Book 10 Upper left section of Pento

Book 10 Upper right section of Pento

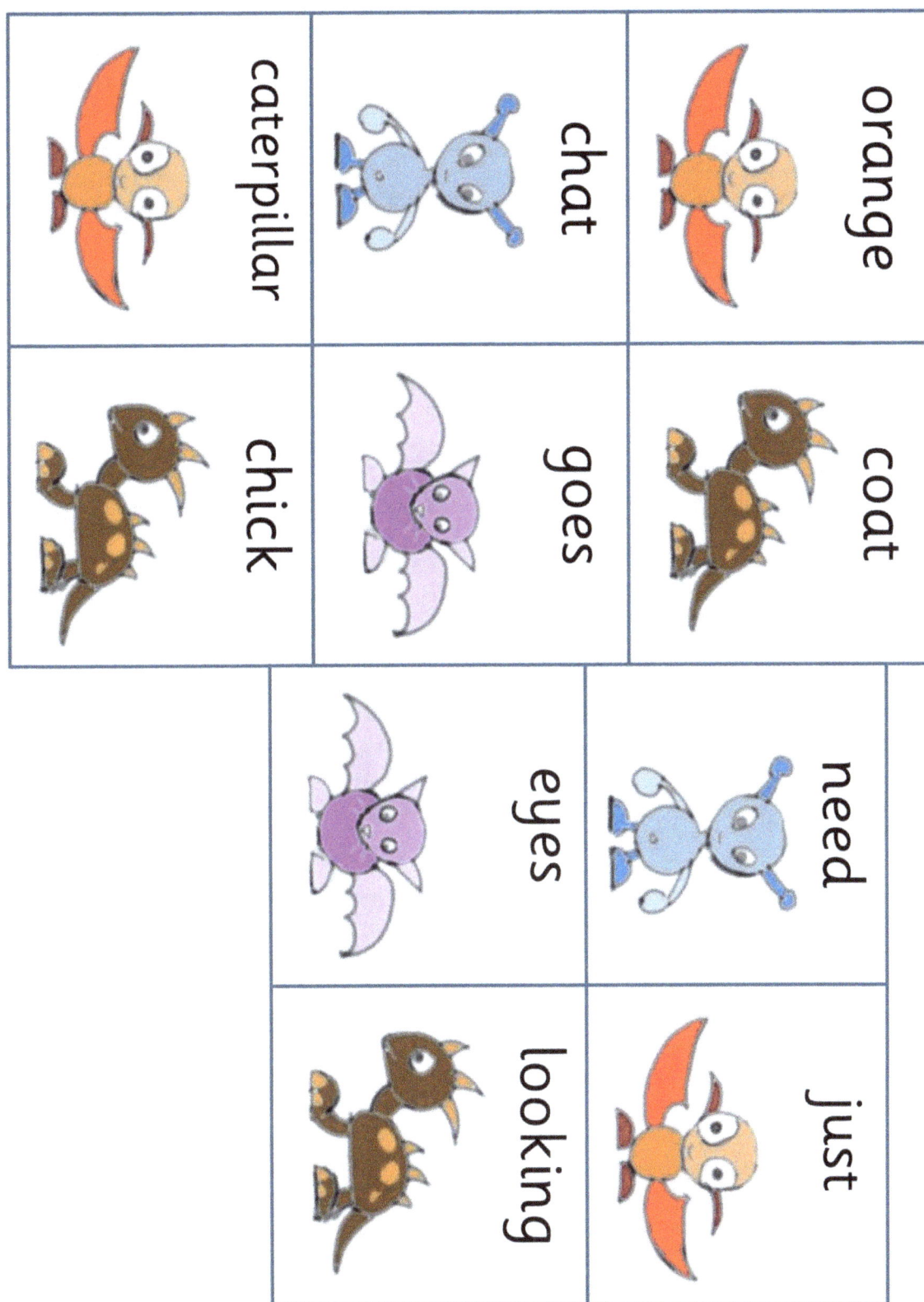

Book 10 Word cards sheet 1 for Pento

Book 10 Word cards sheet 2 for Pento

Cut along bold lines and feed through the window

The robot 11

Word list:

before	buzz	buzzing	flashing	flying
hands	lift	lost	mushroom	next
planet	robot	seen	send	signal
some	three	twinkle	twinkling	what

Targeted phonics:

_oo_
_zz
tw_
fl_

High frequency words:

before
hands
next
some
three
what

Text:
1. The yellow star is twinkling. A ship is flying in the sky.
2. Can you see what is in the flying ship?
3. There is a very small robot in the flying ship.
4. The robot is looking for Zon. The flying ship is going to land by some mushrooms.
5. The mushrooms are in the wood. Tod is upset, he has not seen a robot before.
6. Tod is going to get Grog. Grog will help the robot to look for Zon.
7. Zon is next to his shell. He has seen a robot before. He is from the little planet and the robot is too.
8. The robot tells Grog that he is happy Zon is not lost.
9. The robot tells Zon to go back with him to the little planet. But Zon is happy to stay with the weebees.
10. Now the robot is flashing. His two eyes are flashing. He is going to send a signal to his little planet.
11. Next the robot will buzz. His two hands are buzzing. His eyes will twinkle. He will send two signals to his planet.
12. The robot will tell his planet that Zon is not lost. He will tell them that Zon is happy and will stay with the weebees.
13. The robot goes back to his flying ship. Grog, Tod and Zon go with him.
14. They see the flying ship lift off. Three... two... one... off it goes.

Book 11 Lower left section of Grog's Journey

Book 11 Lower right section of Grog's Journey

Book 11 Upper left section of Grog's Journey

Book 11 Upper right section of Grog's Journey

Book 11 Lower left section for Snakes and Ladders

Book 11 Lower right section for Snakes and Ladders

Book 11 Upper left section for Snakes and Ladders

Book 11 Upper right section for Snakes and Ladders

Book 11 Lower right section of Pento

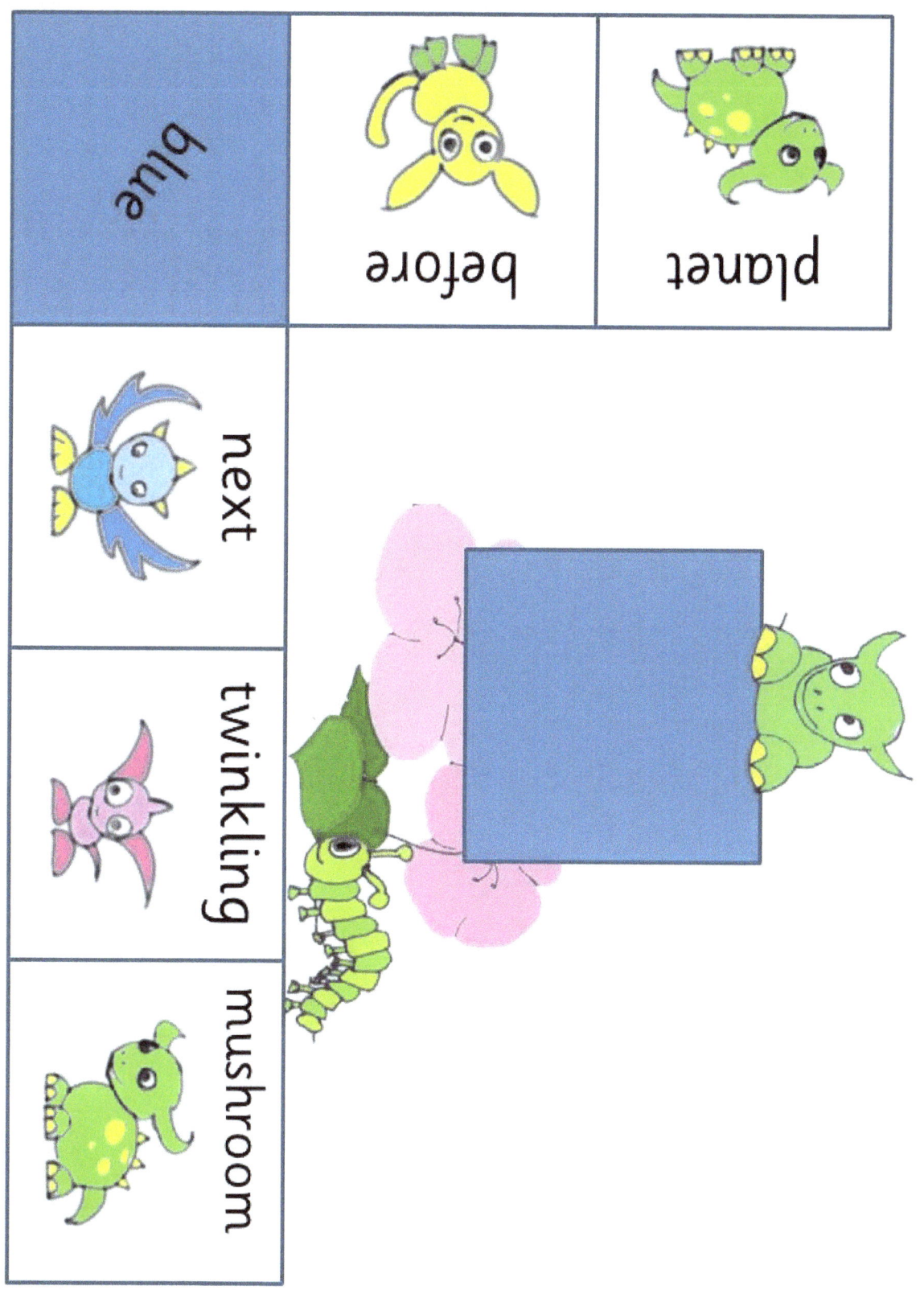

Book 11 Lower left section of Pento

Book 11 Upper right section of Pento

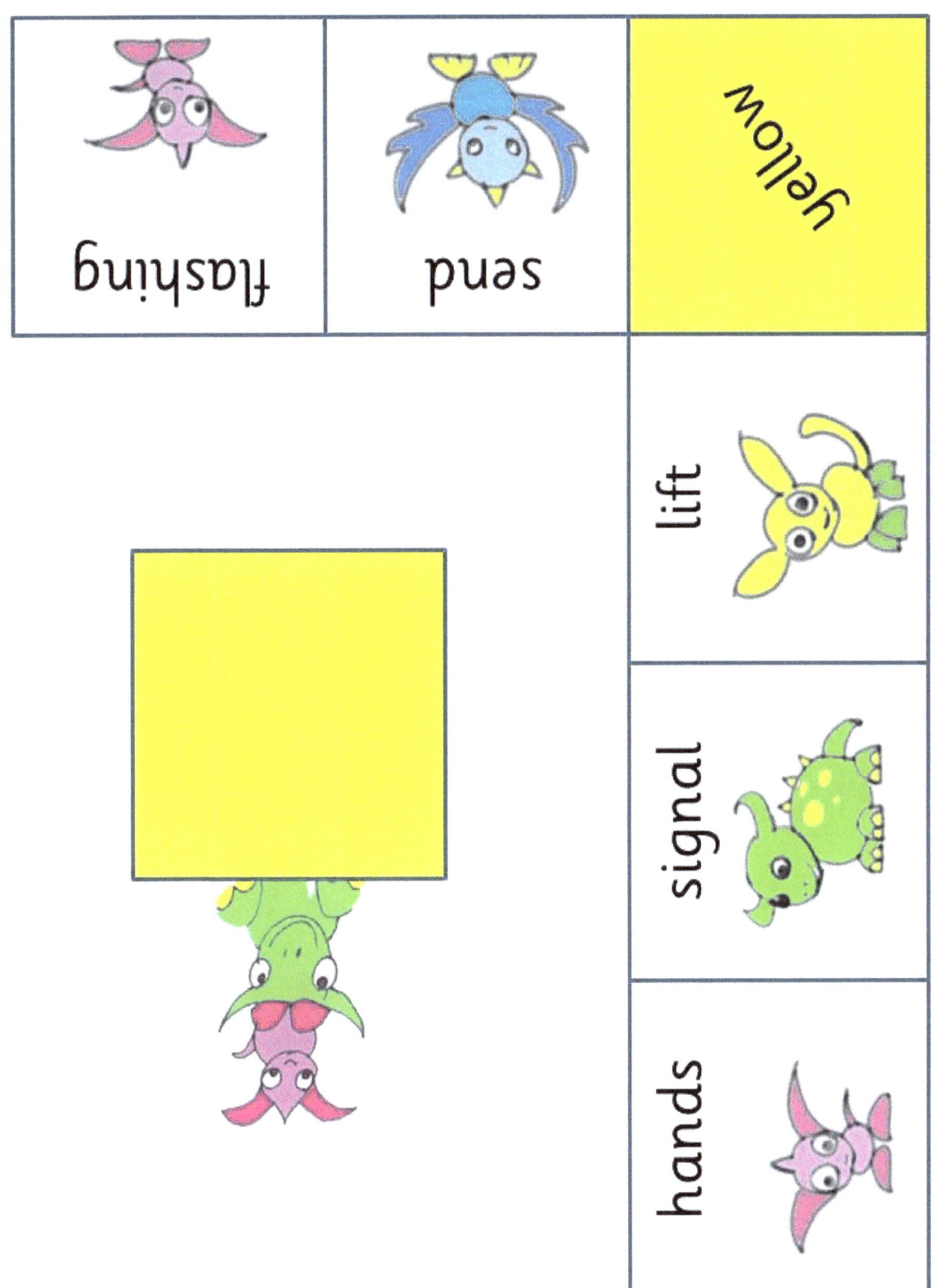

Book 11 Upper left section of Pento

Book 11 Word cards sheet 1 for Pento

Book 11 Word cards sheet 2 for Pento

Cut along bold lines and feed through the window

The Robin 12

Word list:

food	glad	got	hurt	mend
one	pain	quick	rain	robin
seeds	short	shower	splint	then
told	until	was	went	wet

Targeted phonics:

_ow_
_ai
_ur
sh_

High frequency words:

got
one
then
was
went

Text:
1. One day Saff was flying up in the blue sky.
2. Saff was looking for Flup in the wood.
3. Flup was not by the mushrooms. He was not in the wood.
4. Then Saff went to the pond to look for Flup. There was a robin under a big sunflower.
5. The robin was upset. He had hurt his wing. The robin was in pain.
6. Then Flup went to the pond to look for Saff. He saw the robin.
7. Flup went to get Grog. He told Grog that the robin needed help.
8. Grog went to help. He told Saff to get a short stick. He told her to be quick. It was going to rain.
9. Saff got a short stick from the wood. Grog put it on the hurt wing. It was a good splint.
10. Next they all went under the tree to stay dry. The robin was glad that Grog had put the splint on his wing.
11. There was a shower of rain. But they did not get wet.
12. Grog told the robin to stay under the tree. The wing was going to mend.
13. Saff and Flup got food for the robin. They got sunflower seeds.
14. The robin stayed until the wing had mended. Then one day there was no pain. The robin was flying in the blue sky.

Book 12 Lower left section of Grog's Journey

Book 12 Lower right section of Grog's Journey

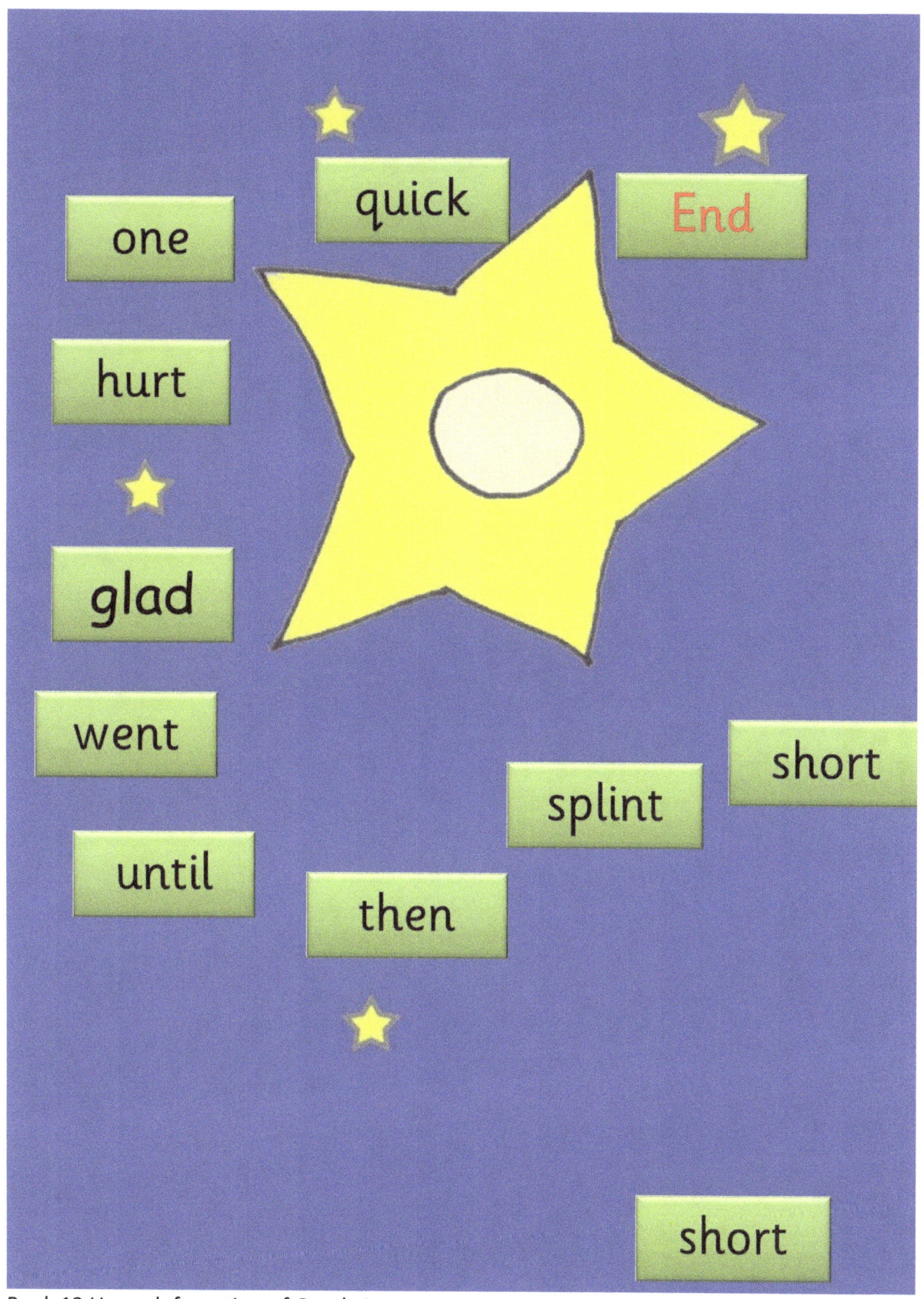

Book 12 Upper left section of Grog's Journey

Book 12 Upper right section of Grog's Journey

Book 12 Lower left section for Snakes and Ladders

Book 12 Lower right section for Snakes and Ladders

Book 12 Upper left section for Snakes and Ladders

Book 12 Upper right section for Snakes and Ladders

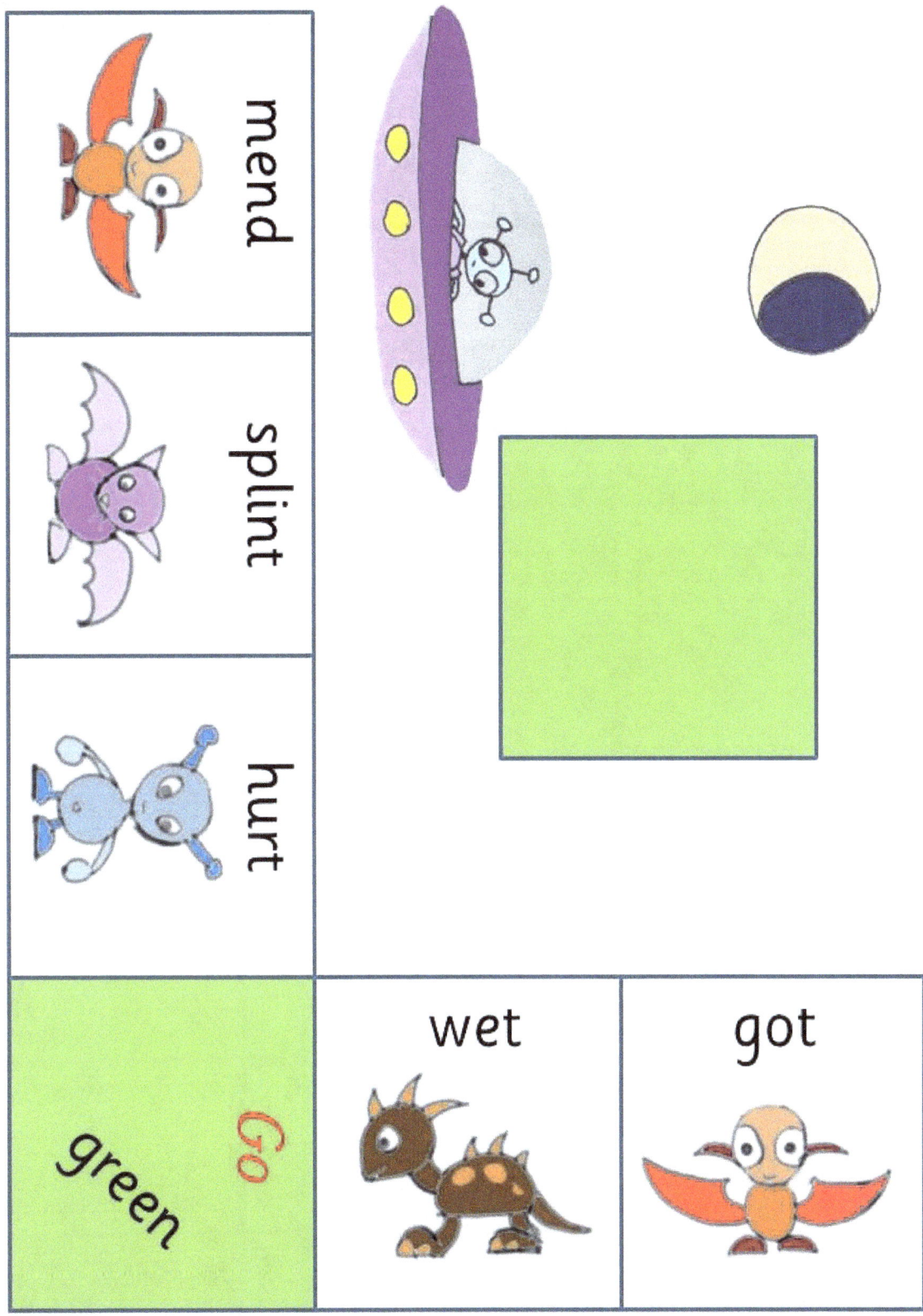

Book 12 Lower right section of Pento

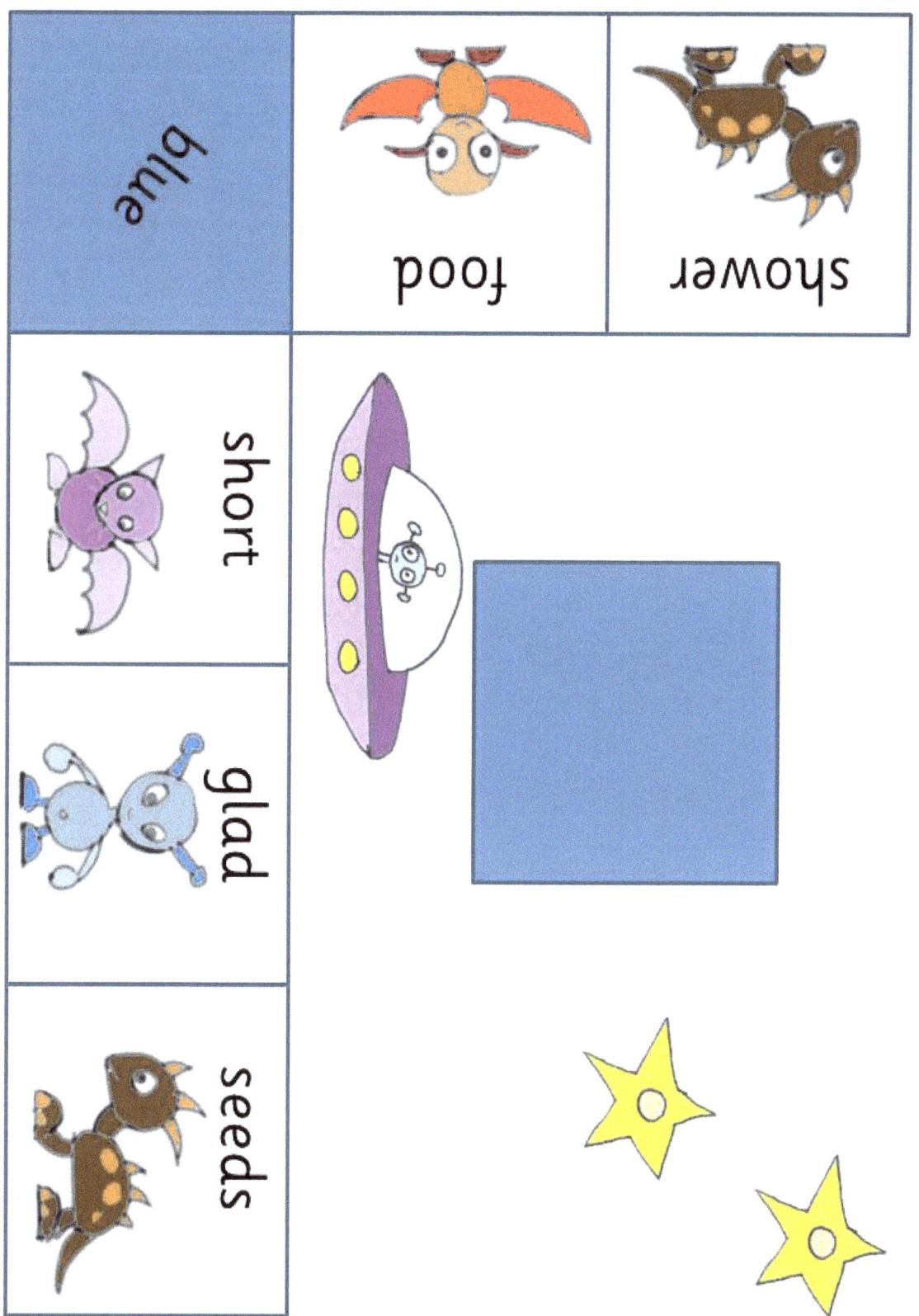

Book 12 Lower left section of Pento

Book 12 Upper right section of Pento

Book 12 Upper left section of Pento

Book 12 Word cards sheet 2 for Pento

Cut along bold lines and feed through the window

The dragon 13

Word list:

come	shook	picnic	lunch	finished
like	said	took	stump	walk
mother	we	bag	sat	saw
home	must	nuts	high	hill

Targeted phonics:
　_y
　_ook
　_gh

High frequency words:

come	like
said	walk
mother	we
bag	saw
home	must
hill	

Text:
1. One day Mop and Pip went on a picnic. They took some food with them.
2. Mop had a bag of nuts and Pip had some seeds.
3. Mop told Tod to come with them for a picnic lunch. Tod was glad to come.
4. There was a tree stump to sit on. They sat down and had some lunch. The sun was high in the blue sky.
5. When they had finished the picnic they went for a walk. They went for a walk next to the pond.
6. Next to the pond they saw a big red hill. Mop, Pip and Tod had not seen the red hill before.
7. The red hill was fun to walk up. It was very high and had big green spots.
8. Just then the red hill shook. "Quick!" said Tod. "We must get off this hill."
9. "Look!" said Mop. "It is a very big dragon. It has green spots like the small dragon from the egg," said Pip.
10. "We must go and get Grog," said Tod. "We must tell Grog that there is a big dragon next to the pond."
11. Grog was with the very small dragon, deep down in the roots of the tree.
12. Tod told Grog that there was a big dragon by the pond. Tod told Grog that it had green spots like the little dragon.
13. "It must be his mother," said Grog. "We must go with the little dragon to look for his mother."
14. The mother dragon was very glad to see the little dragon. She took him back home.

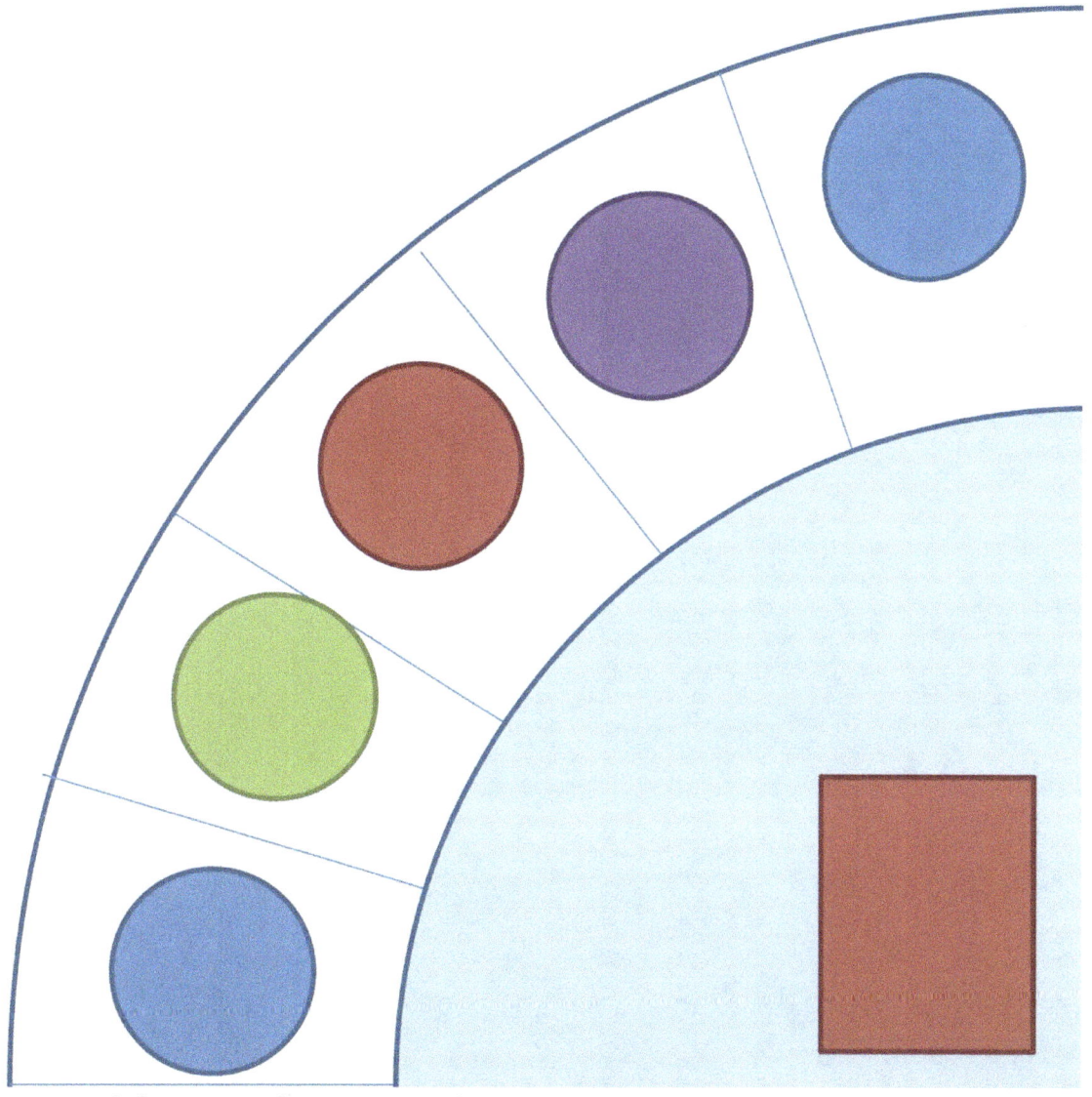

Book 13 Lower left section of Spectro Board

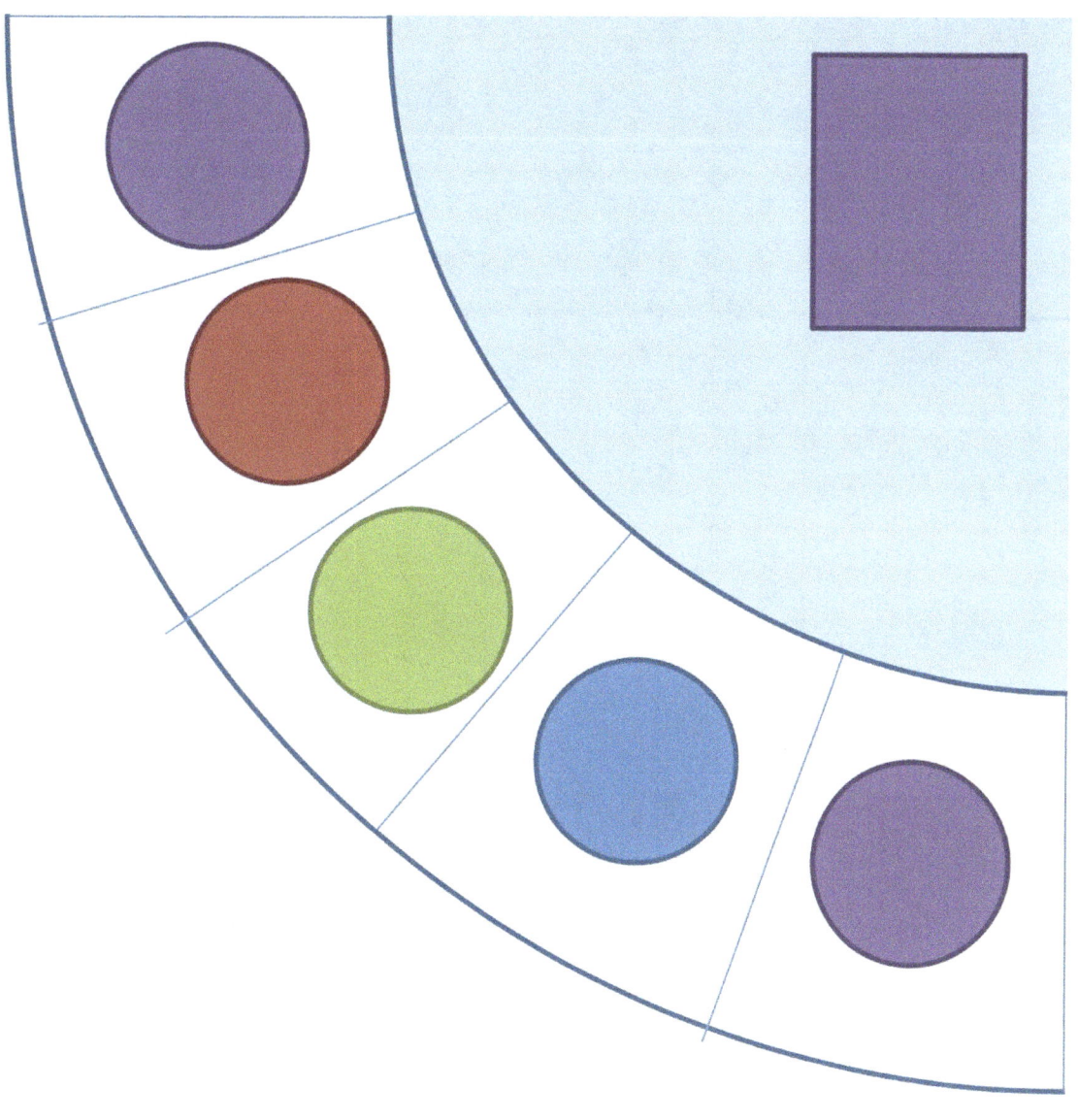

Book 13 Lower right section of Spectro Board

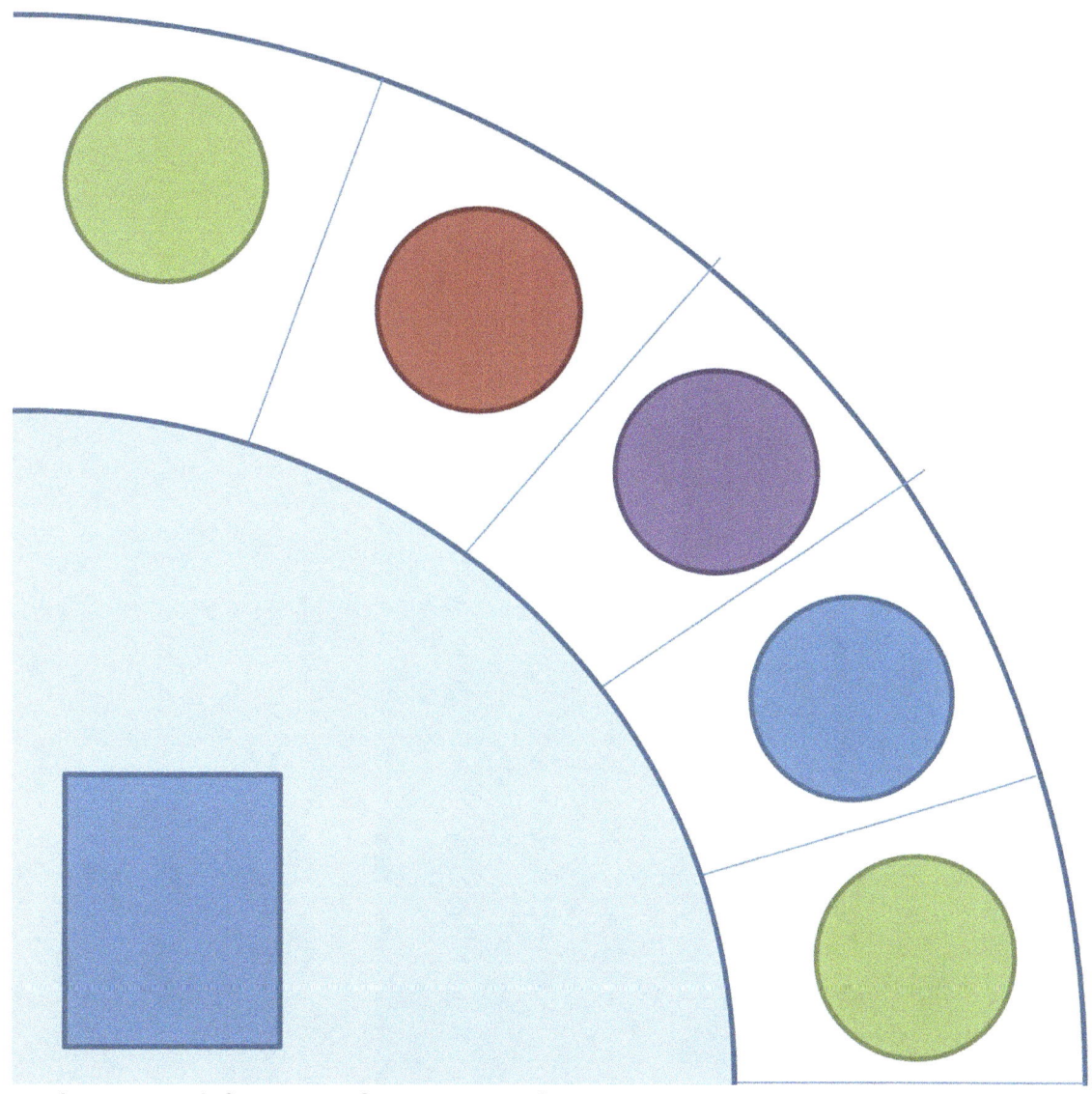

Book 13 Upper left section of Spectro Board

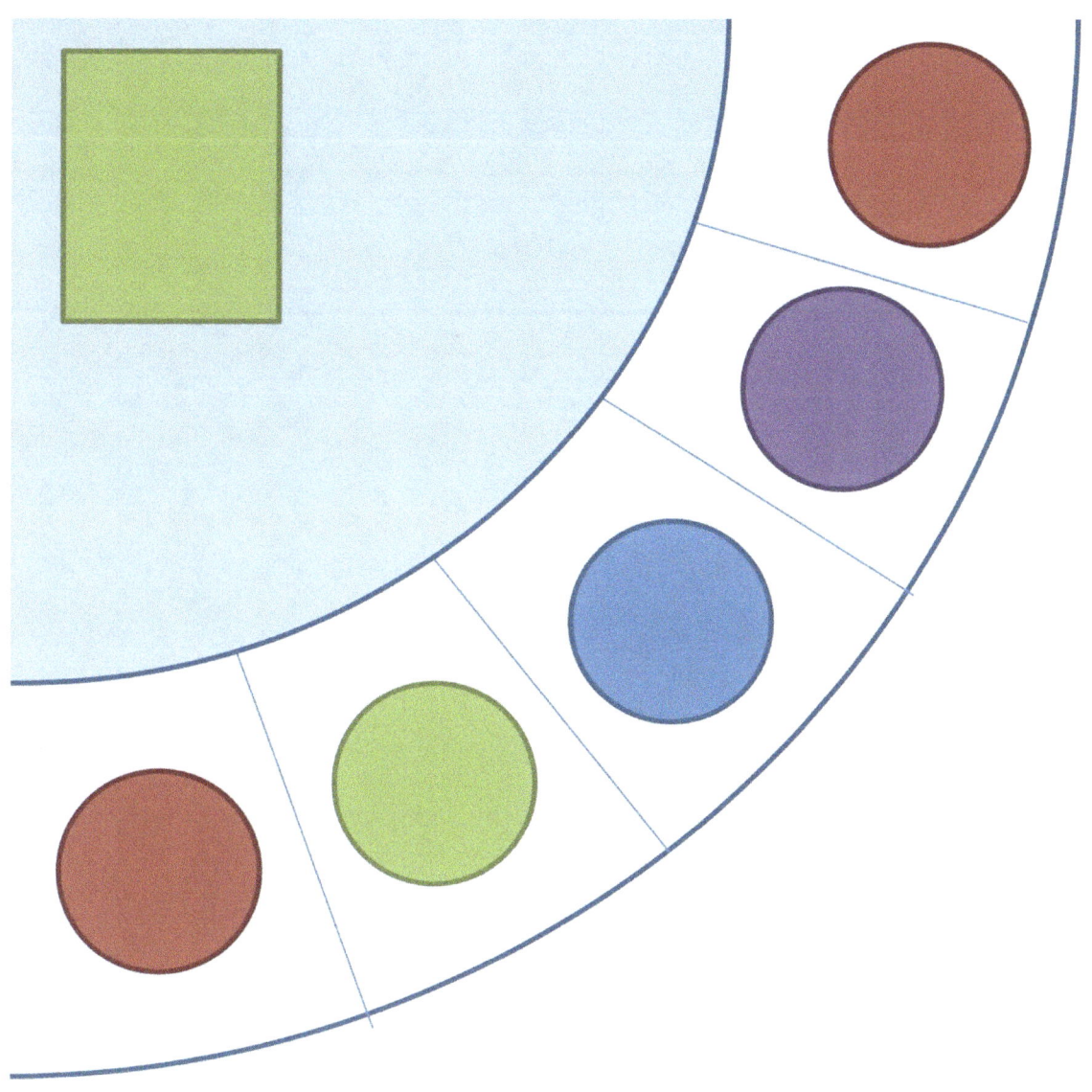

Book 13 Upper right section of Spectro Board

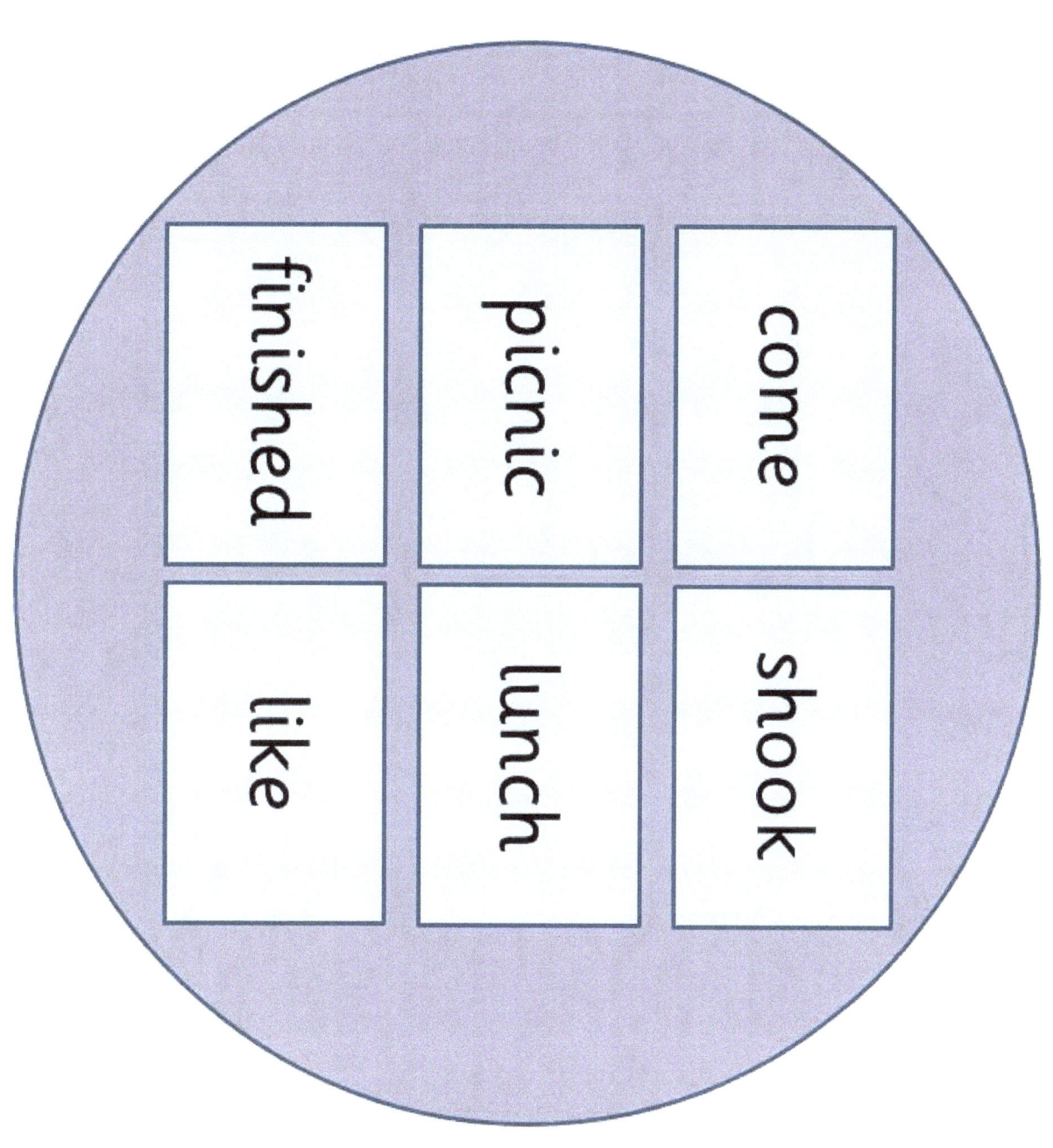

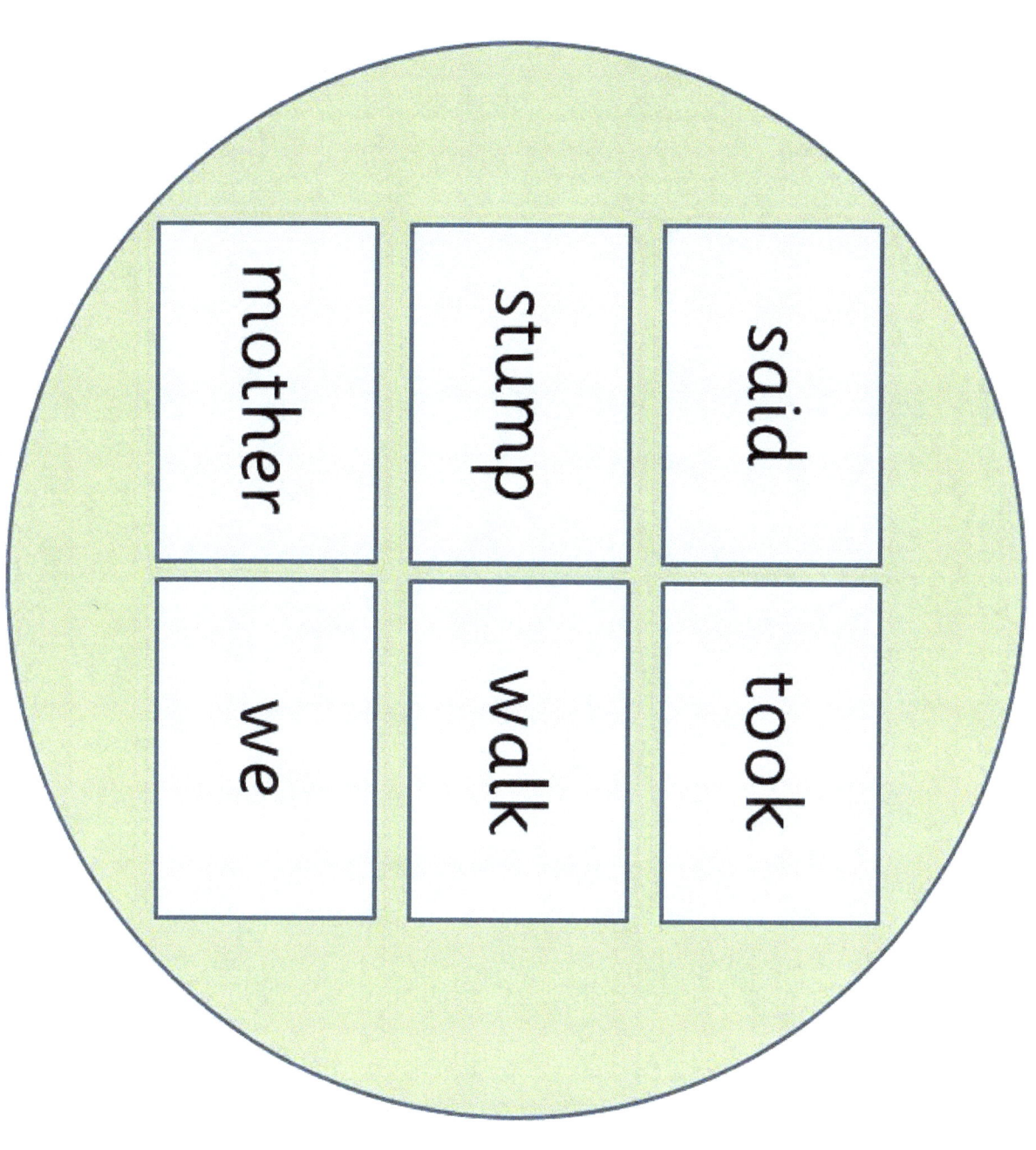

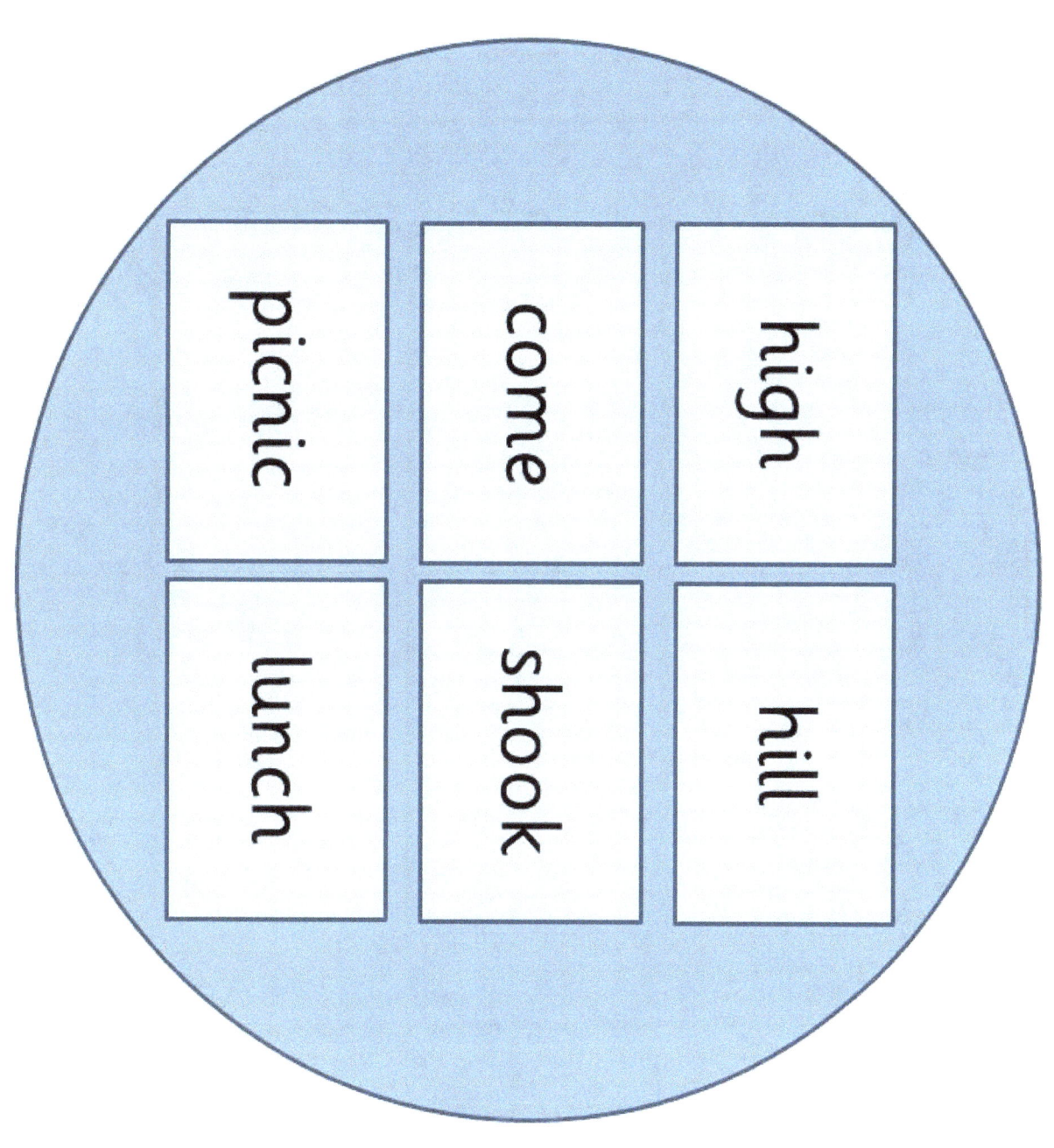

Book 13 Blue board Spectro

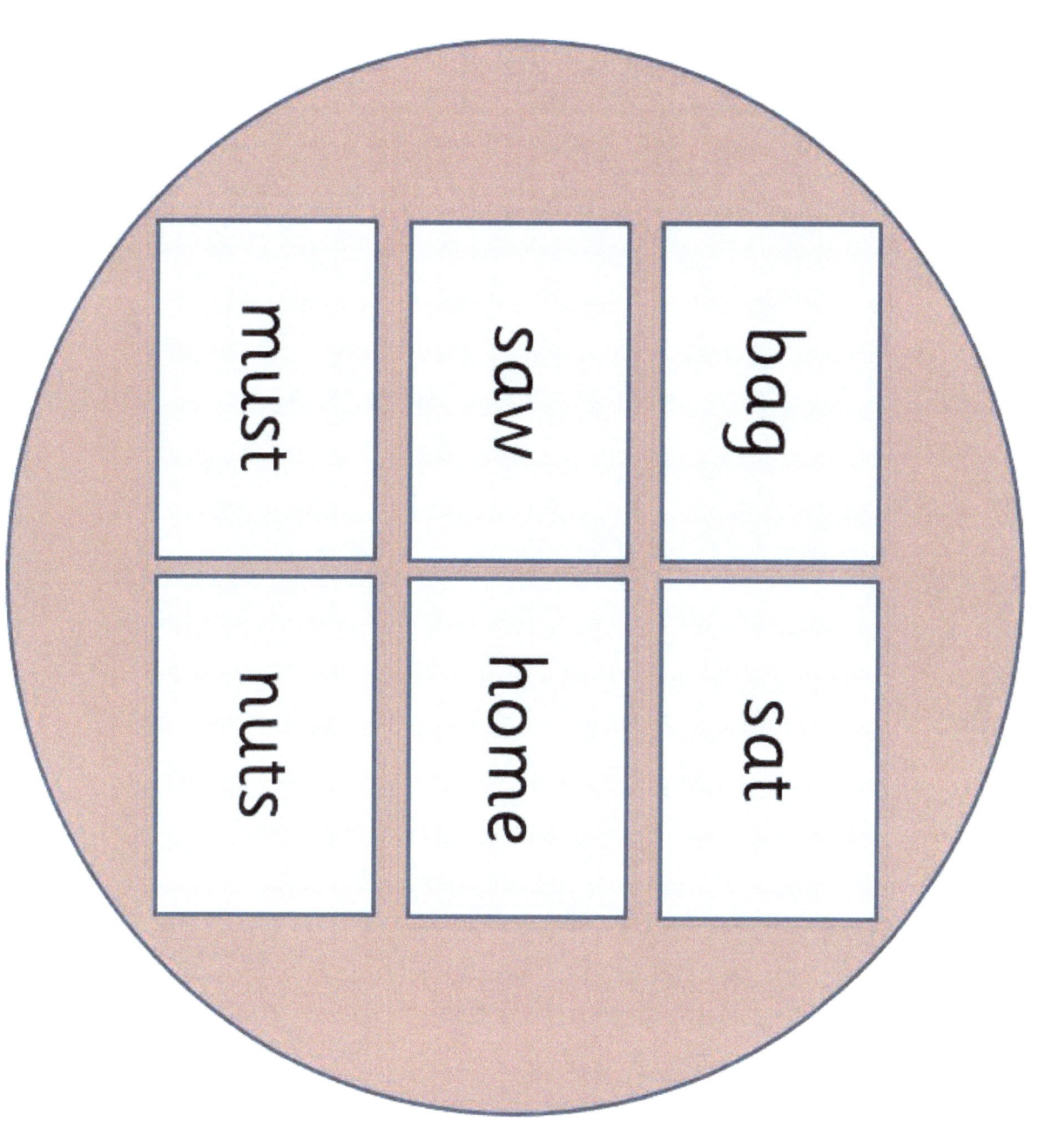

Book 13 Red board Spectro

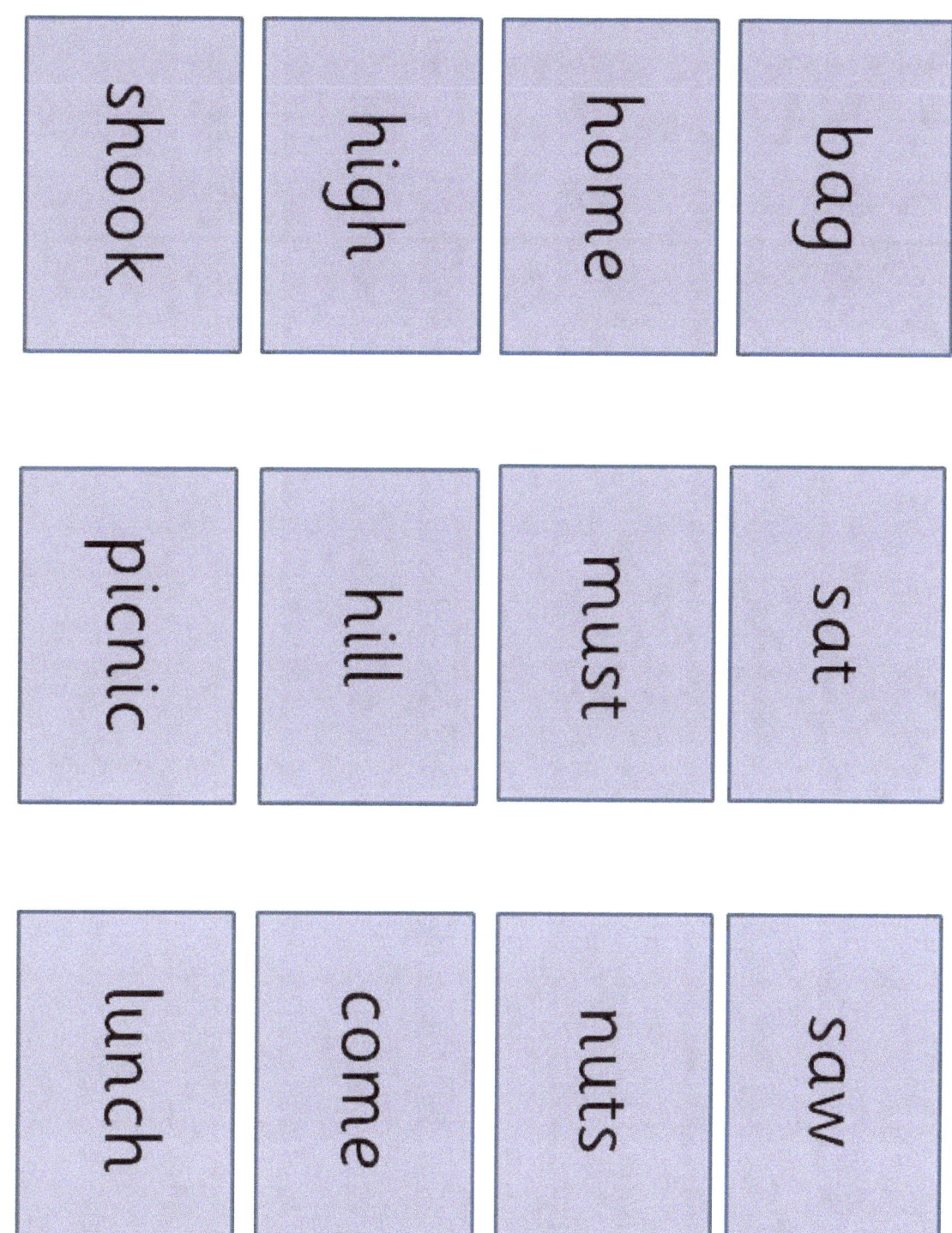

Book 13 Purple words for Spectro. Words to be cut out and stacked on the circular board.

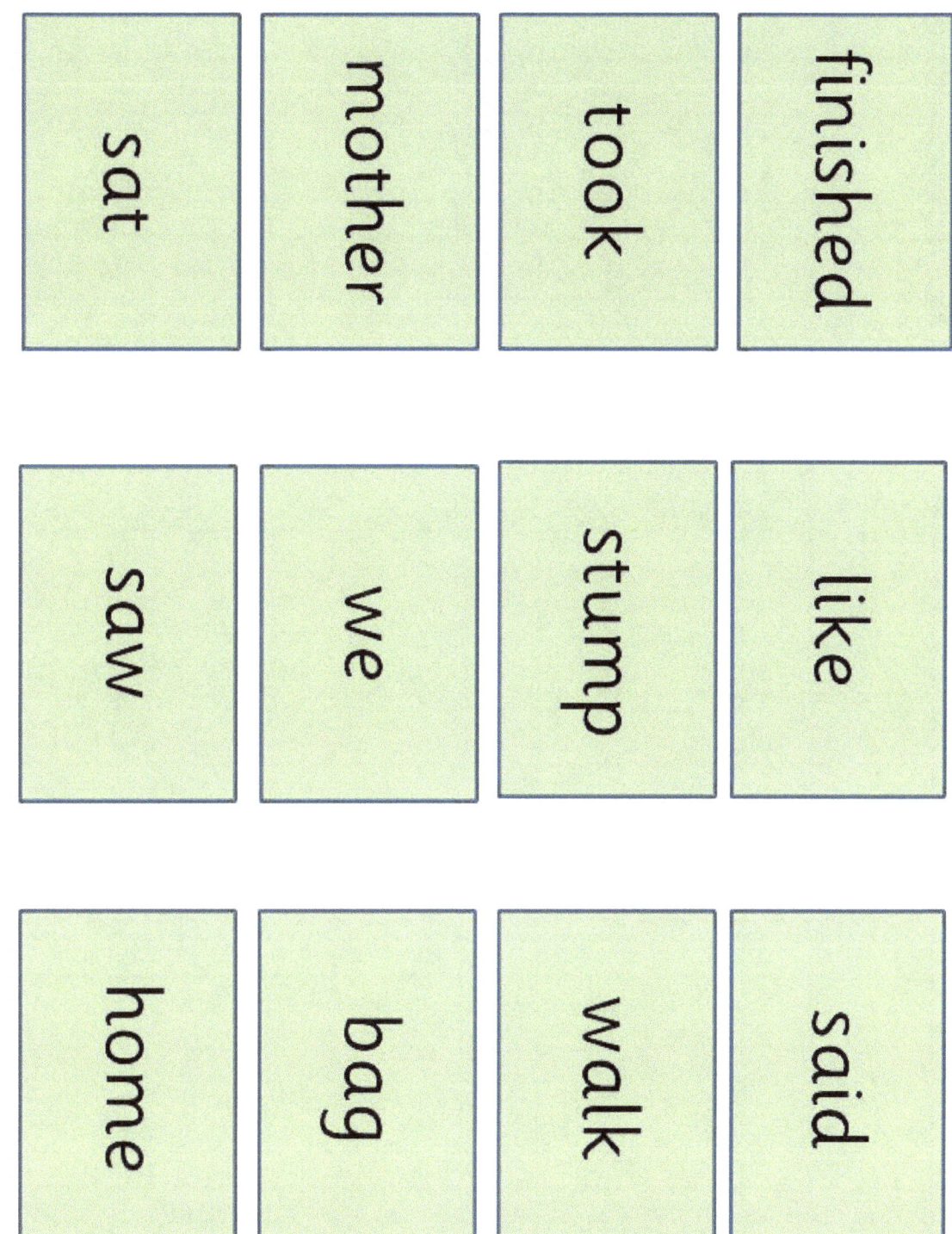

Book 13 Green words for Spectro. Words to be cut out and stacked on the circular board.

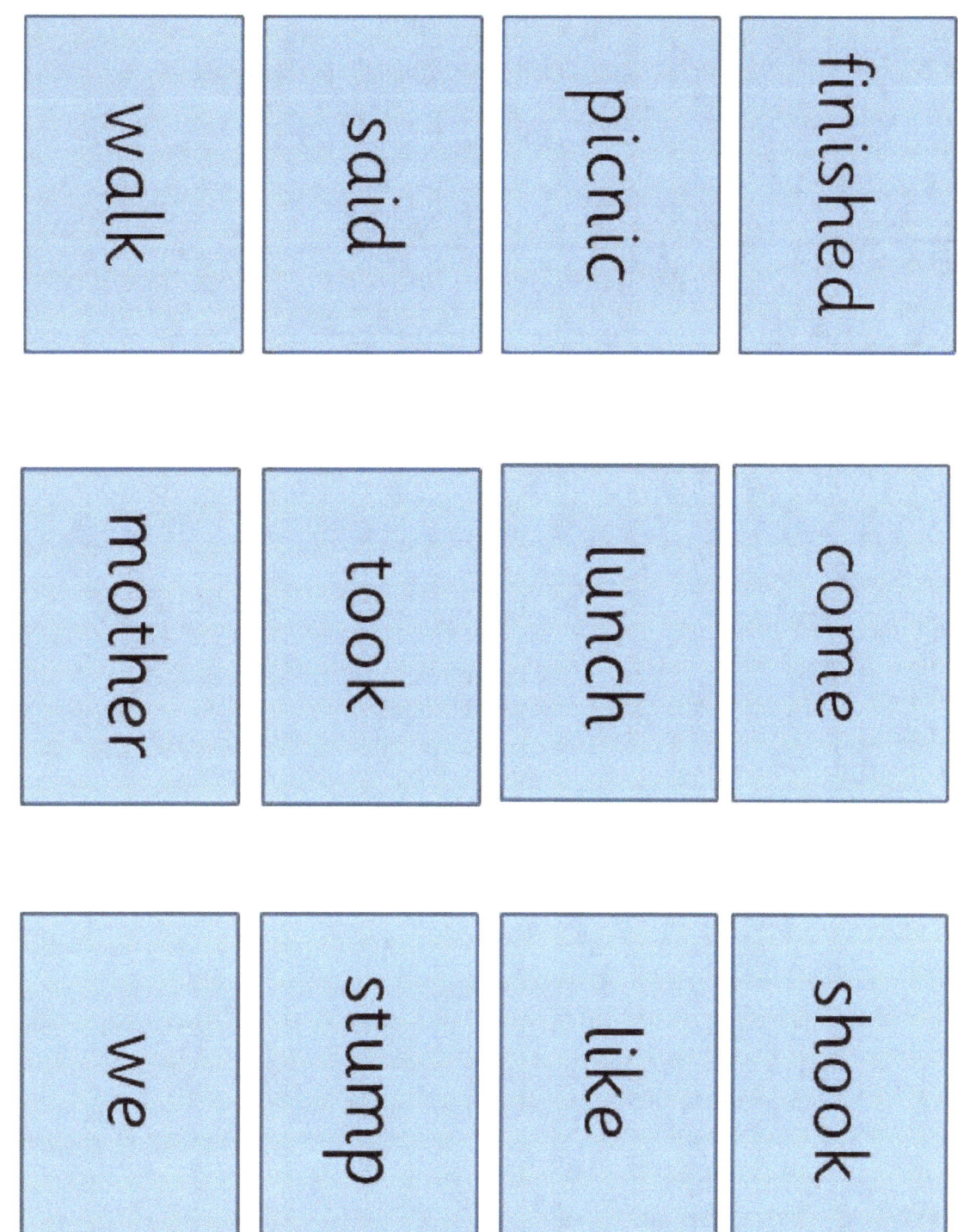

Book 13 Blue words for Spectro. Words to be cut out and stacked on the circular board.

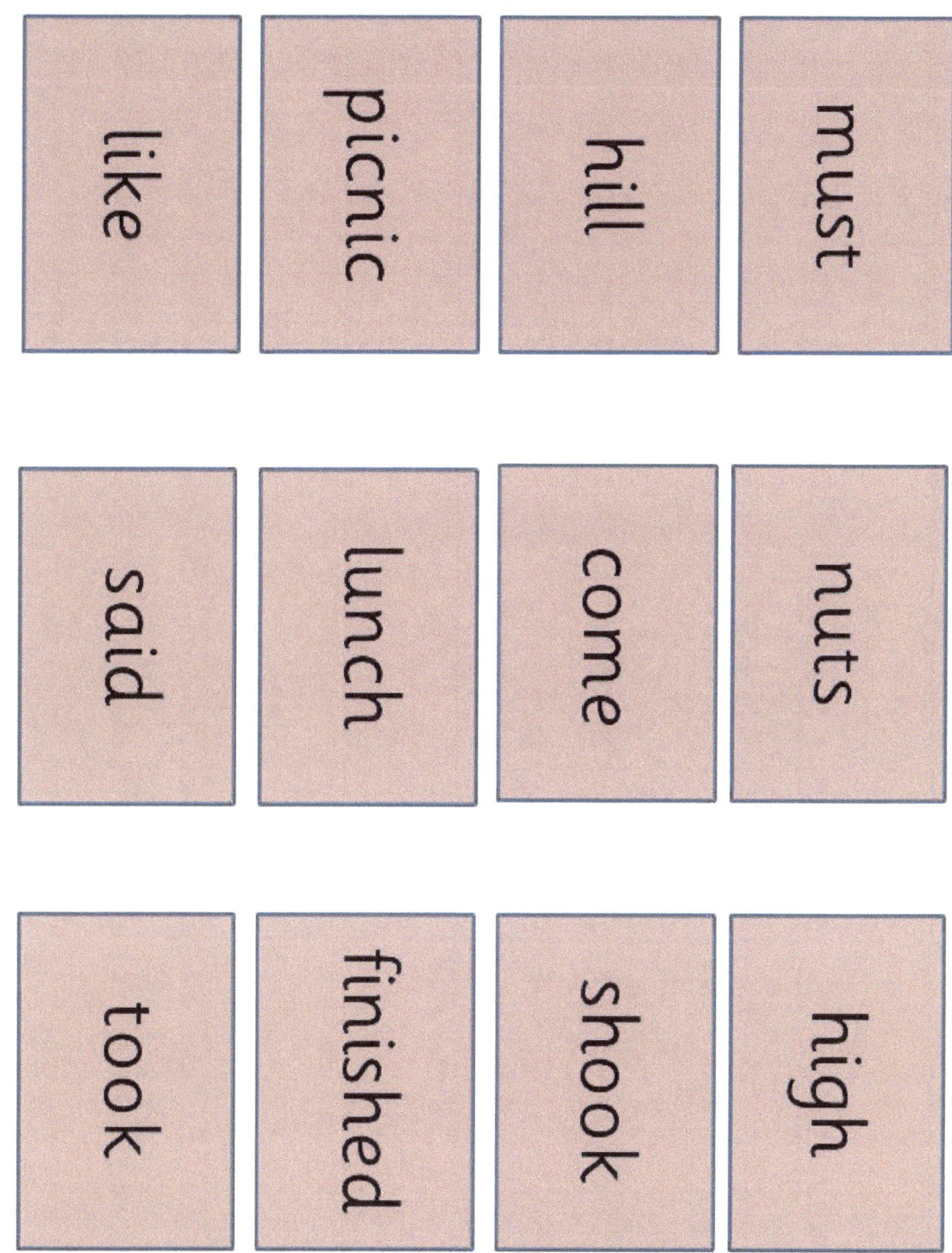

Book 13 Red words for Spectro. Words to be cut out and stacked on the circular board.

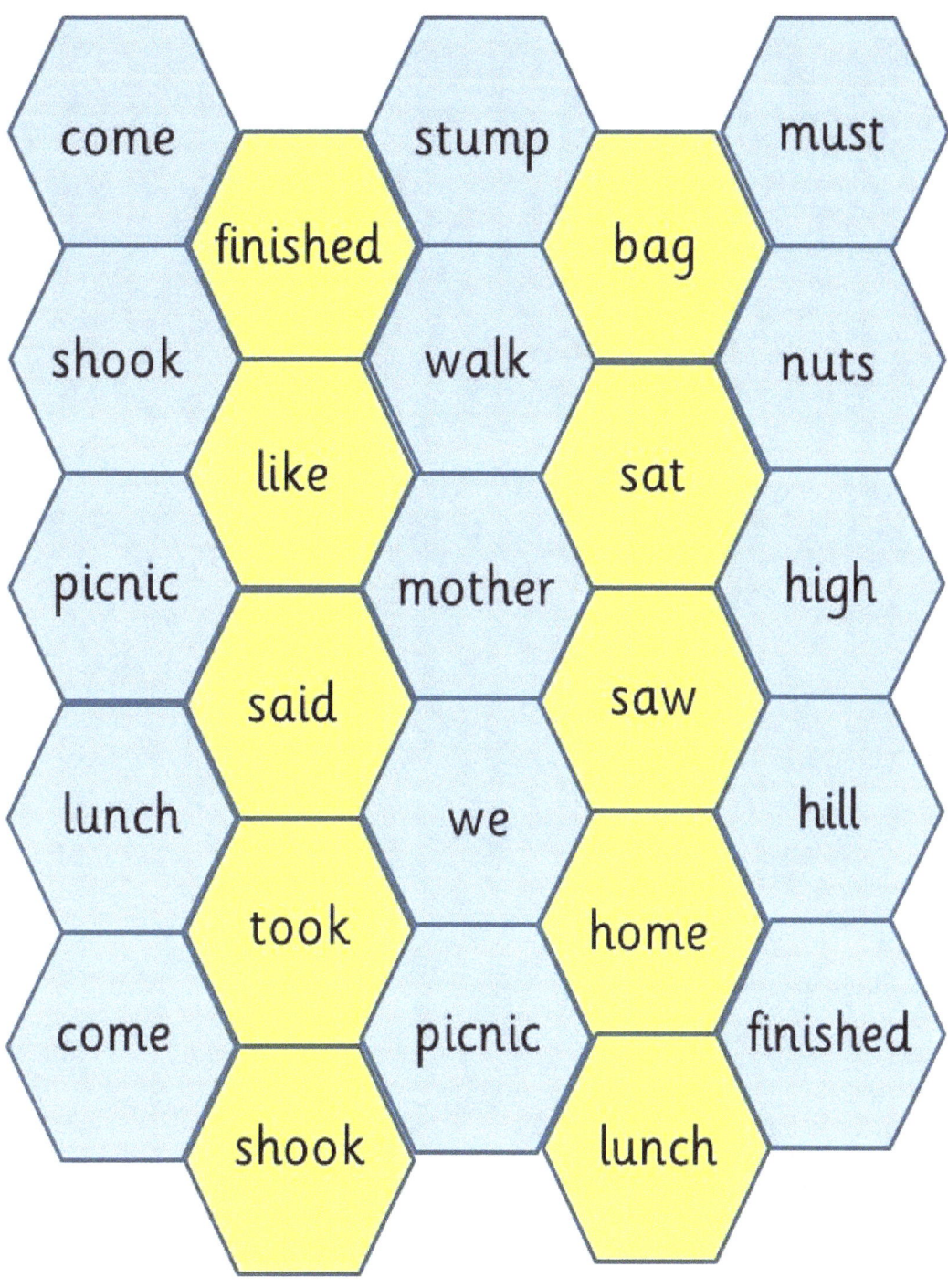

Book 13 Board 2 for Hex Connex

Book 13 Counters to be cut out individually for Hex Connex

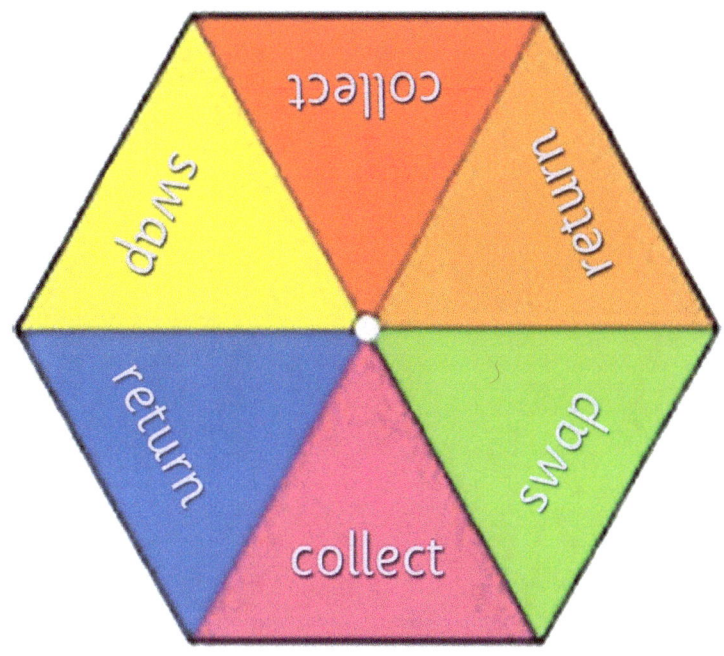

Spinner for Hex Connex

Cut along bold lines and feed through the window

The frog 14

Word list:

were	frog	felt	started	me
hopped	lily	melt	eat	show
much	pad	sent	out	water
my	right	frost	find	thank you

Targeted phonics:
- bl_
- _st
- _lt

High frequency words:

were	me
eat	much
out	water
my	right
find	thank

Text:
1. It was a cool day, just right for flying.
2. Flup and Jig were playing high in the sky.
3. On the top of a hill they saw some frost. It was on the flowers and trees.
4. Then the sun came out and the frost started to melt. Under the frost was a little frog.
5. Flup saw that the little frog was sad and lost. They saw that he felt upset.
6. Flup and Jig went down to help the little frog. 'I can not find my way home', said the frog.
7. Flup sent Jig to look for Grog. 'The little frog must stay wet. He must not get too dry,' said Flup.
8. Grog was going out to find some mushrooms for lunch. The nuts were much too small to eat. Grog went to the wood to look for food.
9. Jig saw Grog by the mushrooms. 'Flup sent me to find you,' she said. 'We are going to help a little frog find his way home.'
10. 'Come with me,' said Grog. 'I will show you his home. It is by the pond.'
11. Jig went with Grog to the pond. 'Look,' said Grog. 'That is his home. It is a water lily. He can sit on the lily pad.'
12. Jig went back to the hill to find Flup and the little frog. Jig told them what Grog had said.
13. Flup and Jig took the little frog to the pond.
14. Now the little frog felt happy. 'Thank you,' he said as he hopped onto the lily pad.

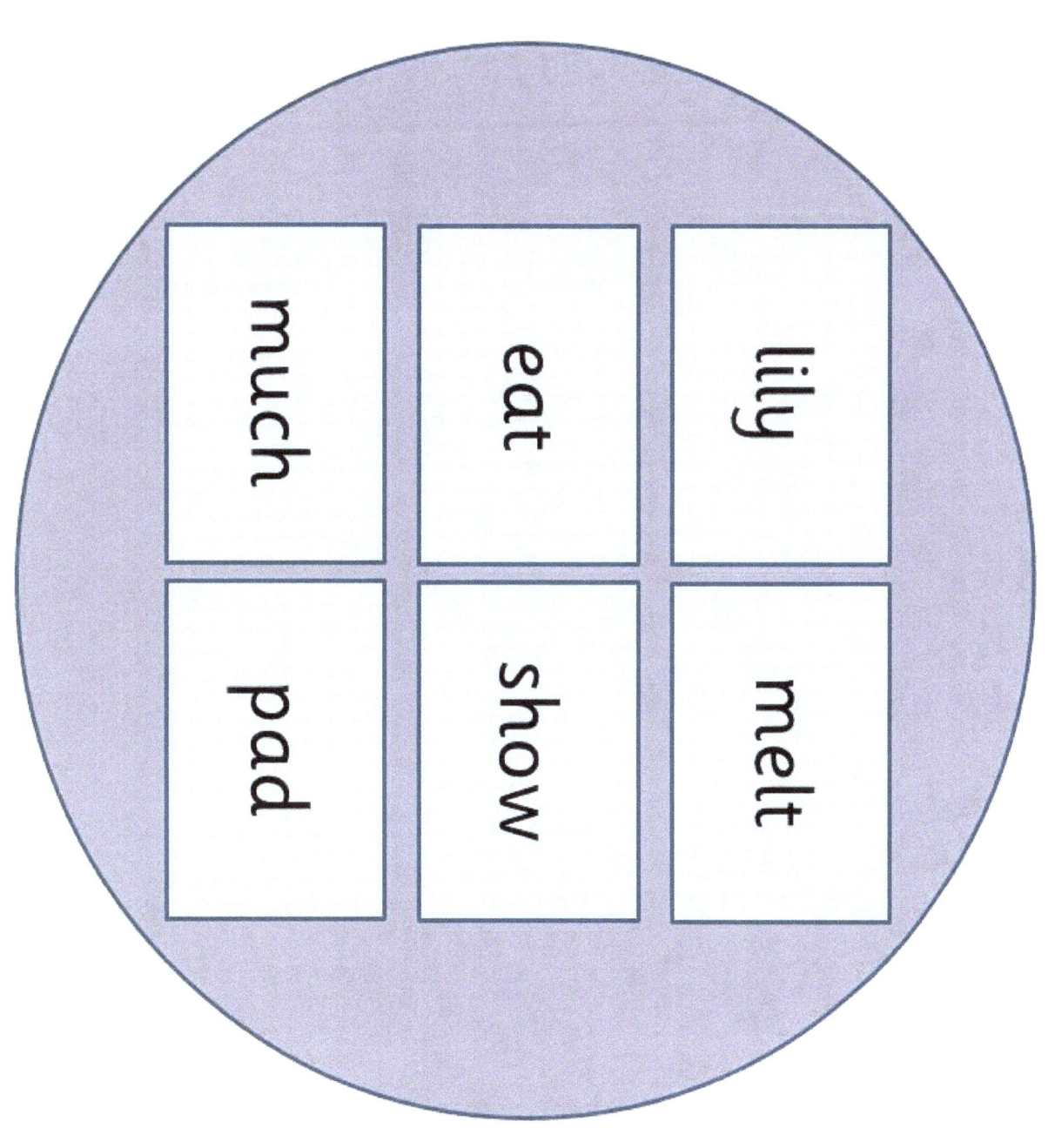

Book 14 Purple board Spectro

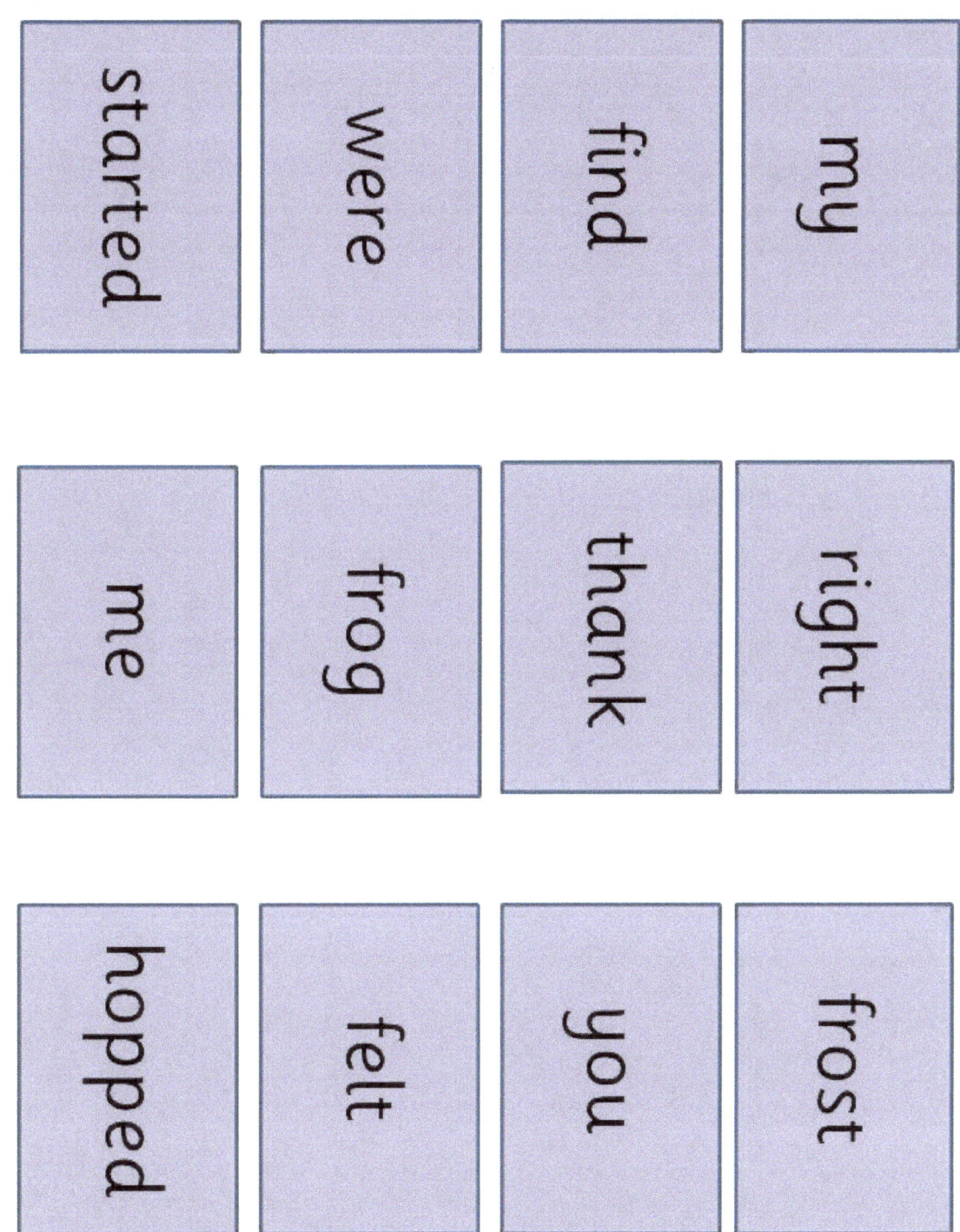

Book 14 Purple words for Spectro. Words to be cut out and stacked on the circular board.

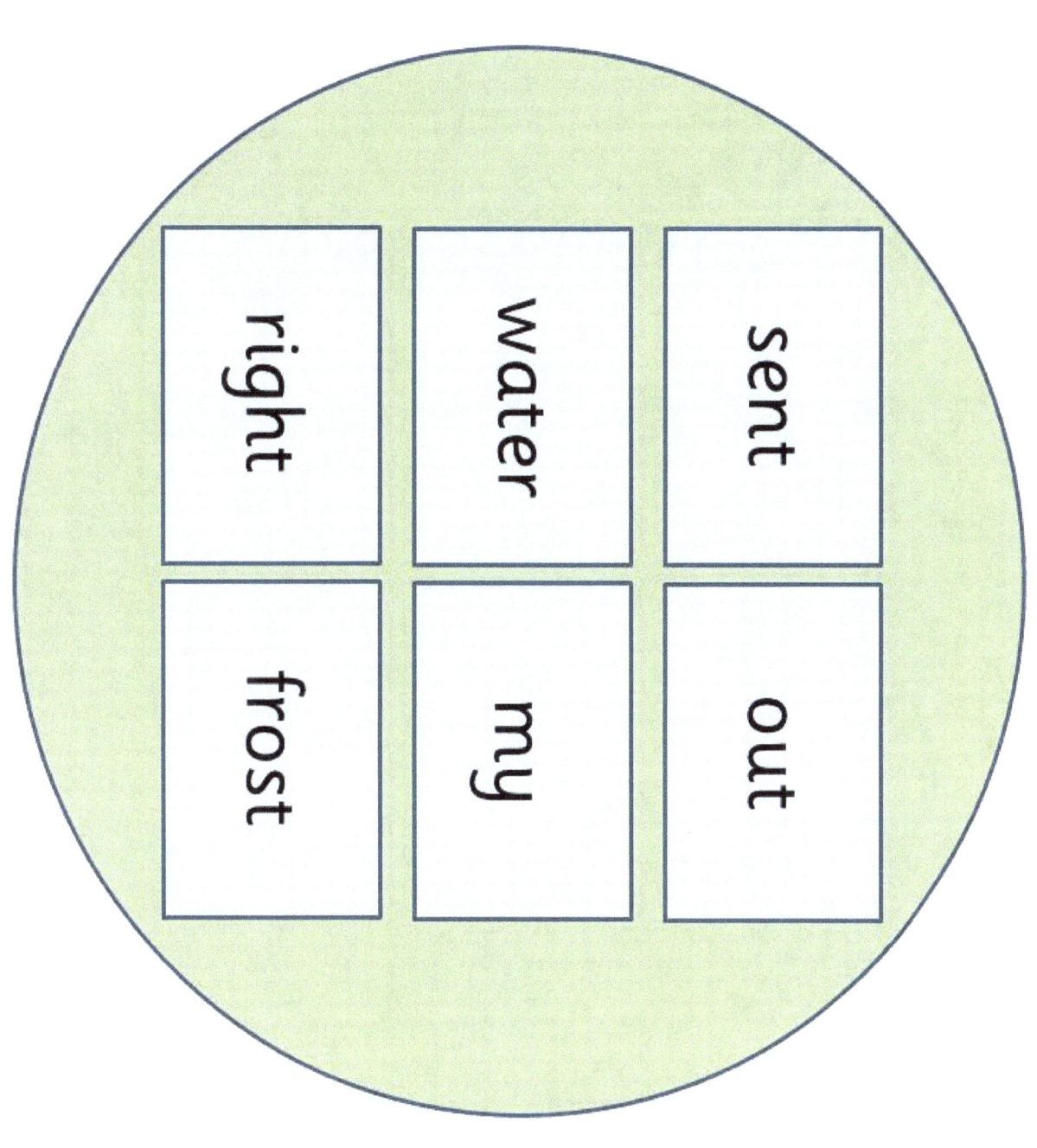

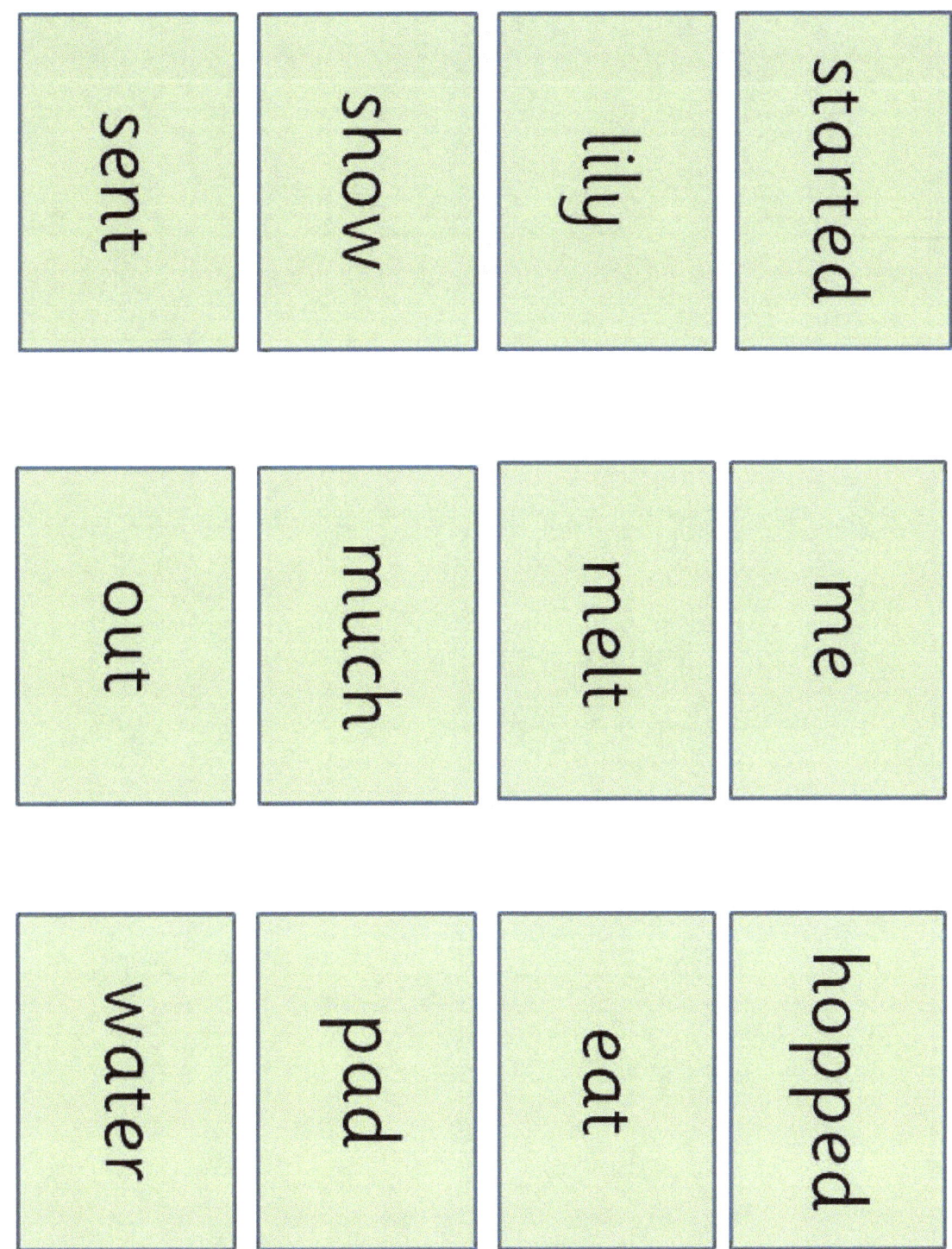

Book 14 Green words for Spectro. Words to be cut out and stacked on the circular board.

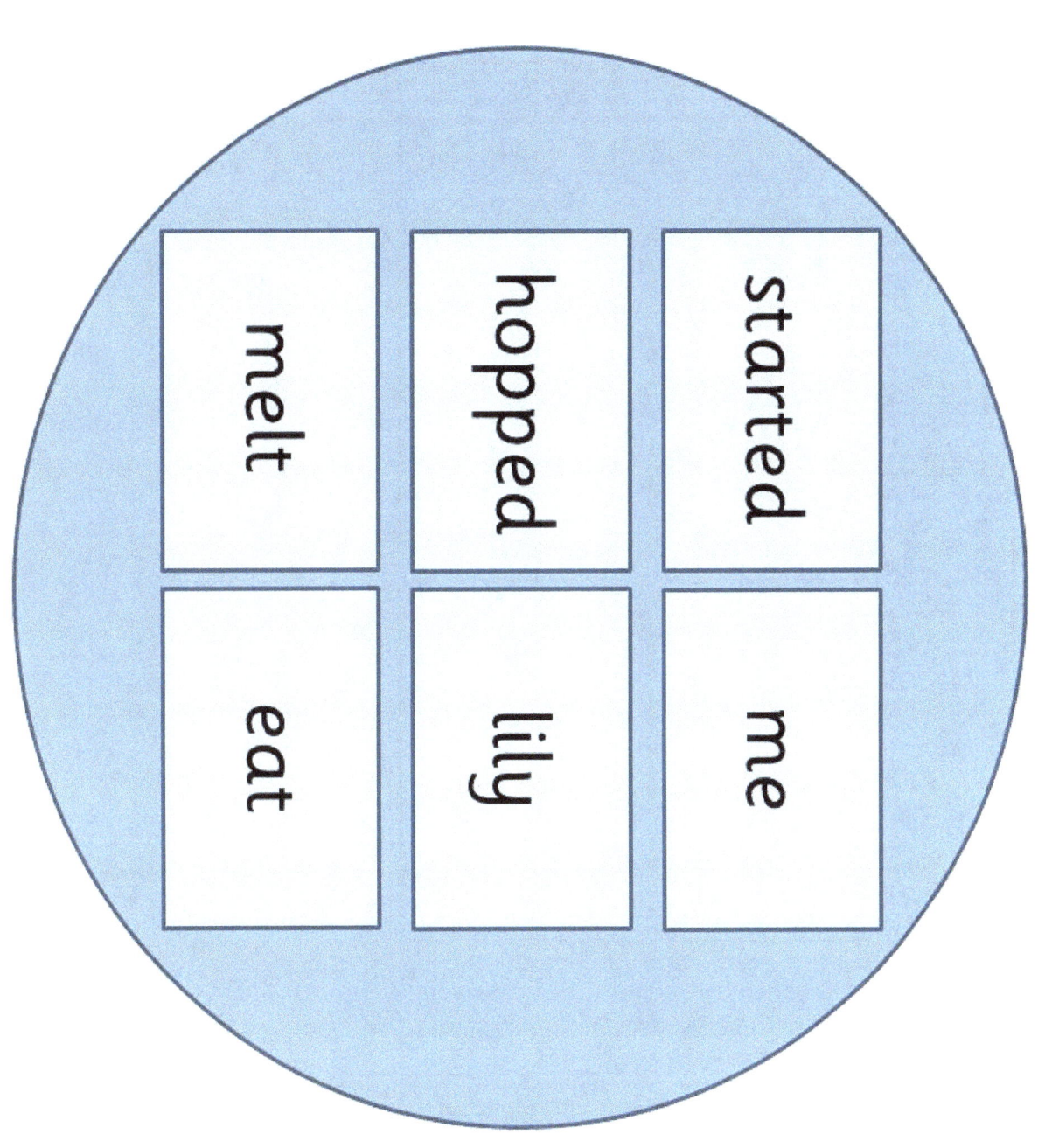

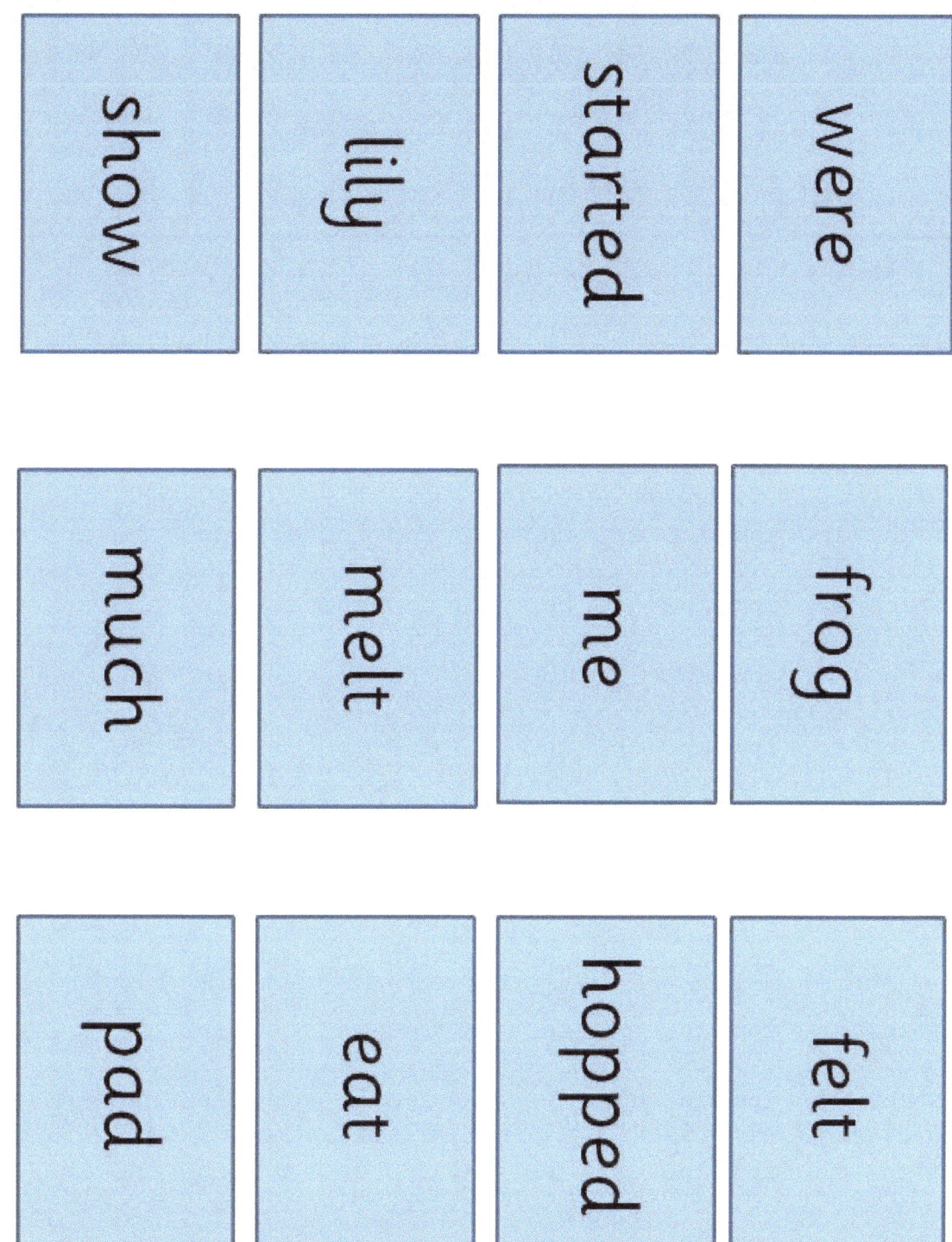

Book 14 Blue words for Spectro. Words to be cut out and stacked on the circular board.

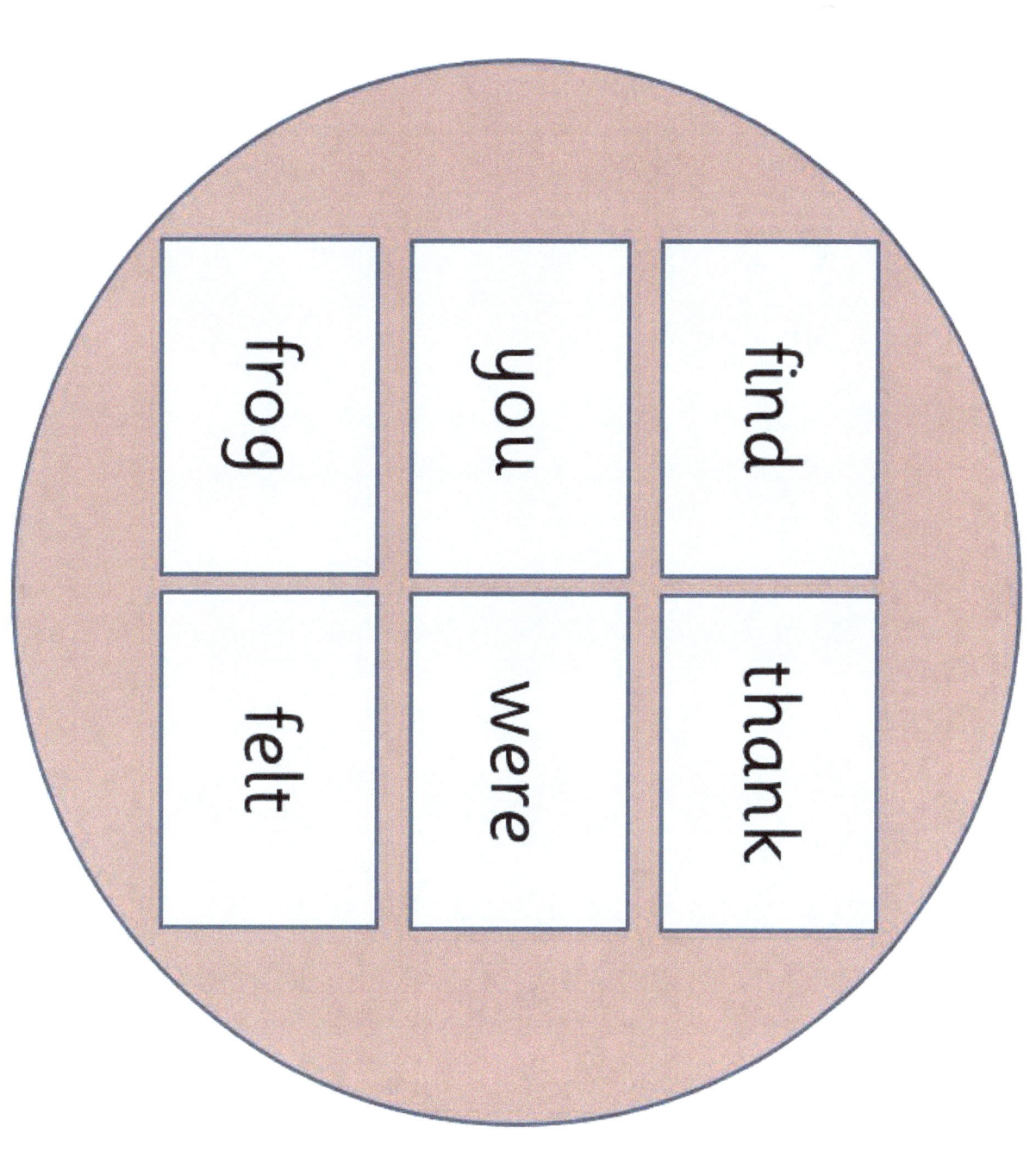

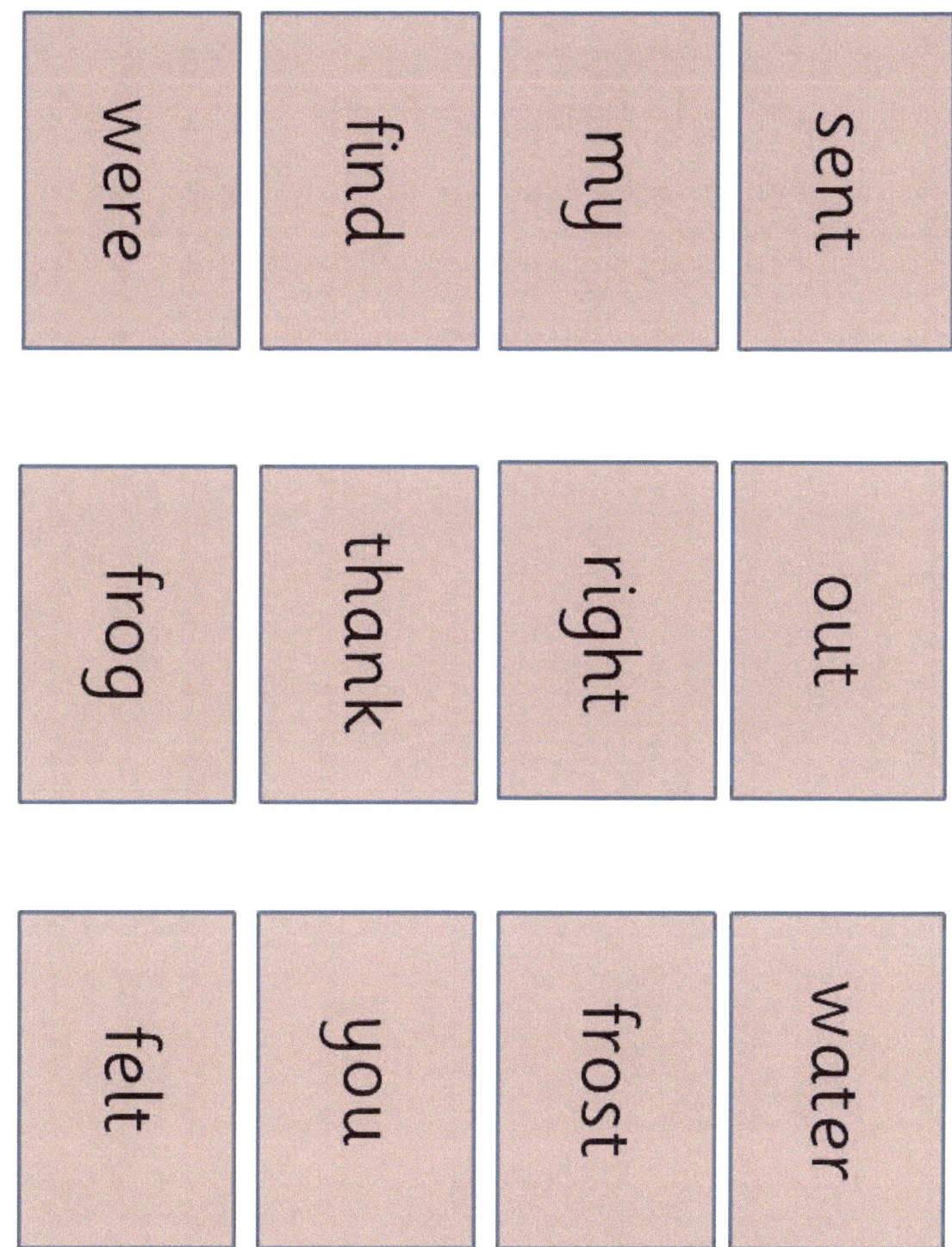

Book 14 Red words for Spectro. Words to be cut out and stacked on the circular board.

Book 14 Board 1 for Hex Connex

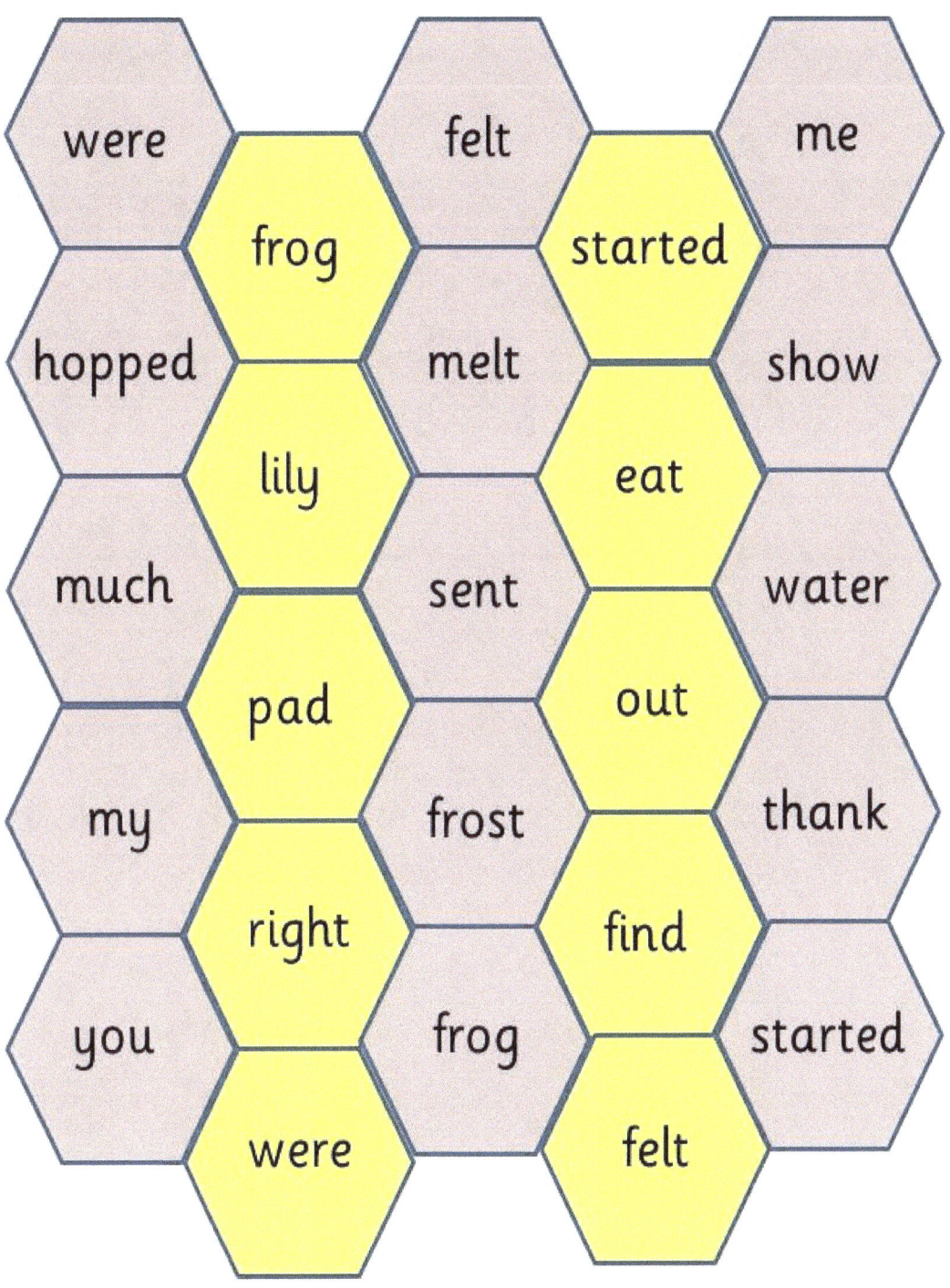

Book 14 Counters to be cut out individually for Hex Connex

Cut along bold lines and feed through the window

The troll 15

Word list:

walked	woods	across	field	bridge
cross	troll	rest	where	do
am	asked	I	want	hear
over	jumped	looked	scary	scared

Targeted phonics:
- ch_
- _ld
- _ll
- _ed

High frequency words:

where	do
am	asked
I	want
over	walked

Text:
1. One day, Grog, Pip, Tod and Zon went for a long walk.
2. They walked to the woods and then to the old wall. Next they walked across the yellow field.
3. When they got to the little bridge they sat down to rest. 'Where do we go now?' asked Zon. 'I want to cross the bridge,' said Grog.
4. Grog, Pip, Tod and Zon did not see the troll under the bridge. They did not hear him. The troll was very cross.
5. 'I want to go over the bridge too,' said Tod. They all went to the bridge.
6. Up jumped the troll. He was very cross. He looked very scary. 'You can not come across my bridge,' said the troll.
7. It is a scary monster.' said Zon. 'Did you hear what he said?' asked Pip. 'I am not scared.' said Grog.
8. 'What will you do to me?' asked Grog. 'I will put you in the water,' said the troll. Pip, Tod and Zon were scared of the troll. Grog was not scared.
9. 'I will cross over the bridge,' said Grog. Zon was scared. He did not want to look.
10. The troll was very small. He was not scary but he looked very cross. 'Where do you want to go?' asked the troll. 'Just into the next field to have a rest before we go home,' said Grog.
11. The troll went into the field with Grog. Pip, Tod and Zon walked over the bridge.
12. They all sat in the field for a rest. The troll told Grog that he did not have a home.
13. Grog asked the troll to go home with him. The troll was very happy.
14. They all walked back home.

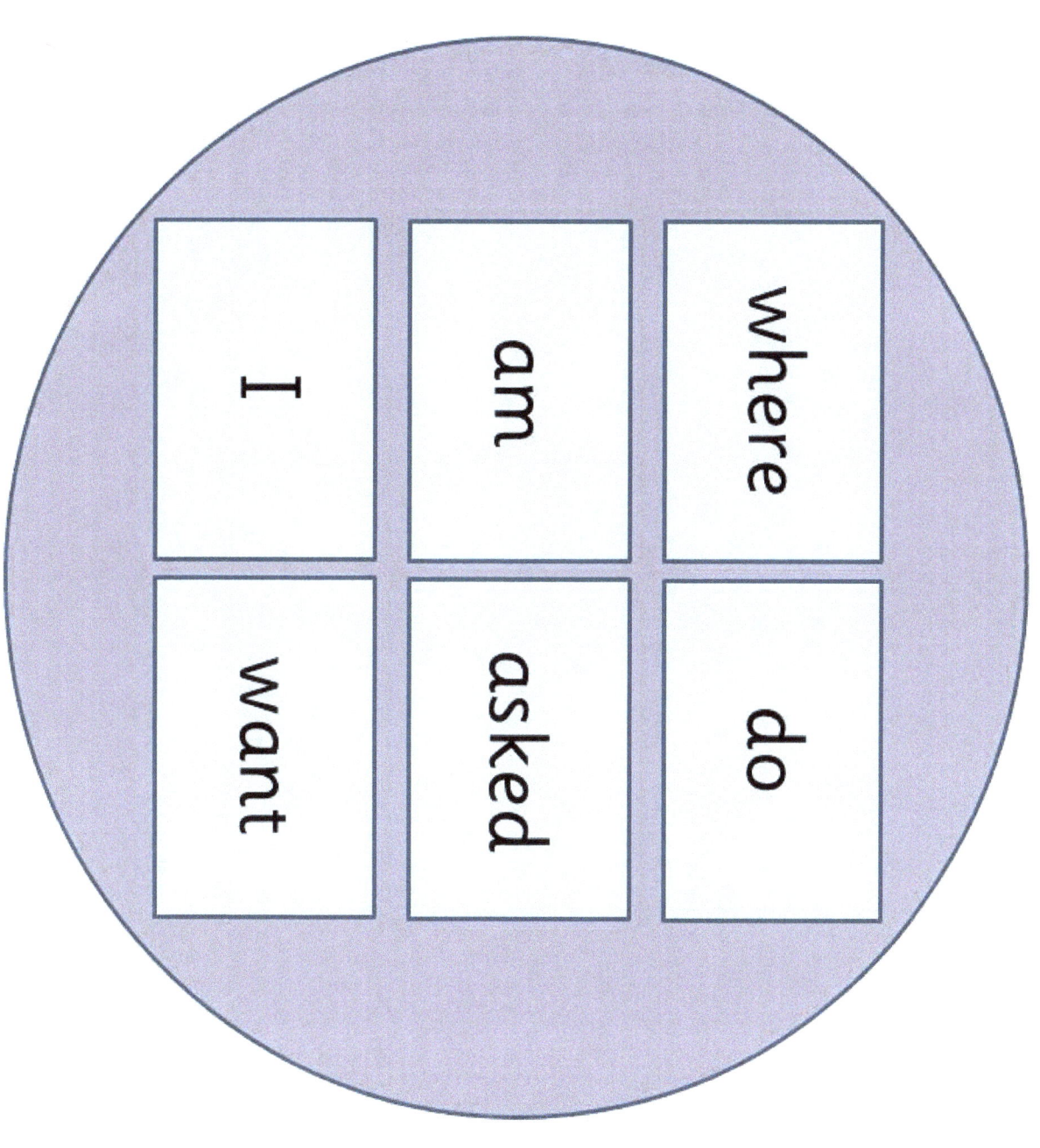

Book 15 Purple board Spectro

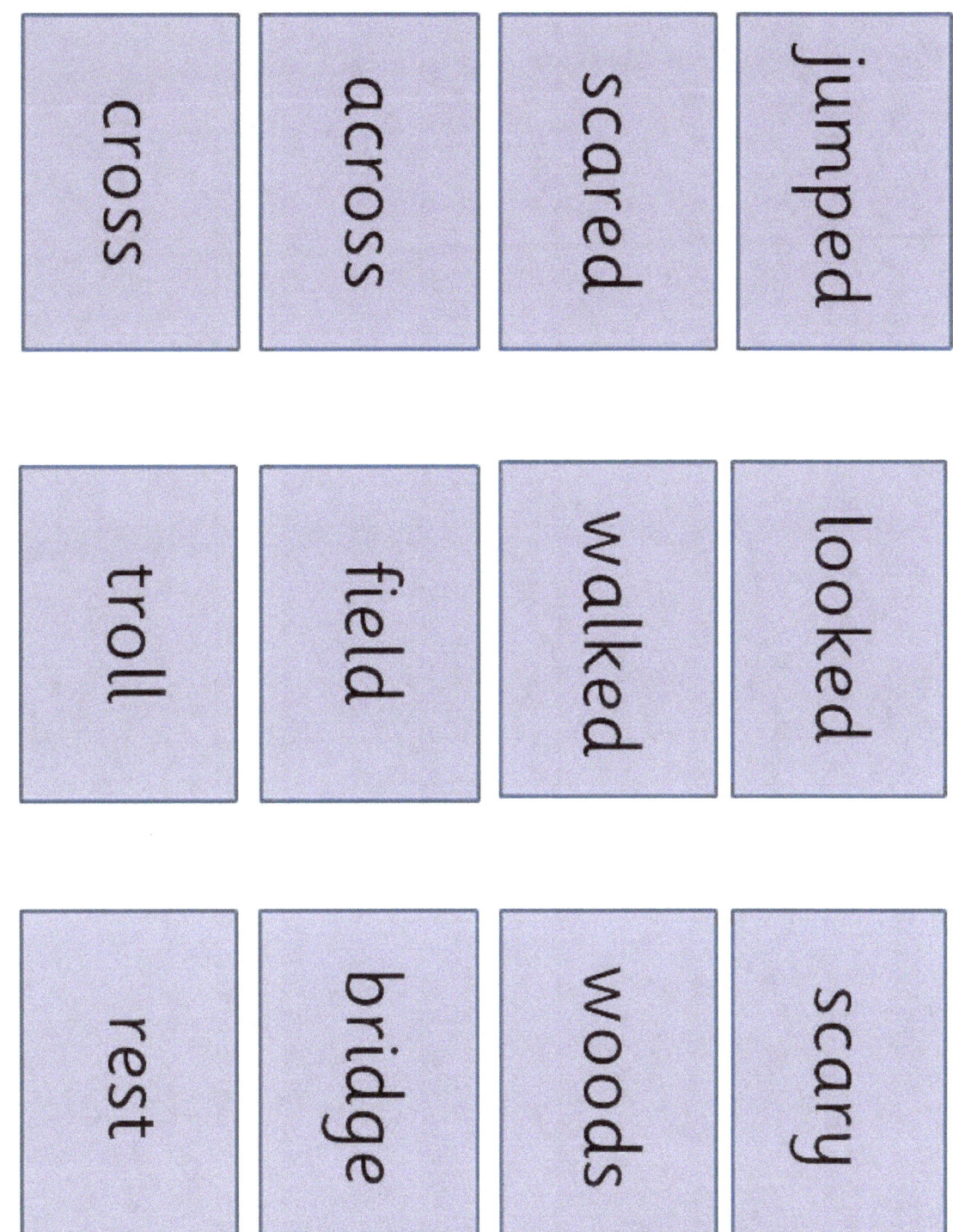

Book 15 Purple words for Spectro. Words to be cut out and stacked on the circular board.

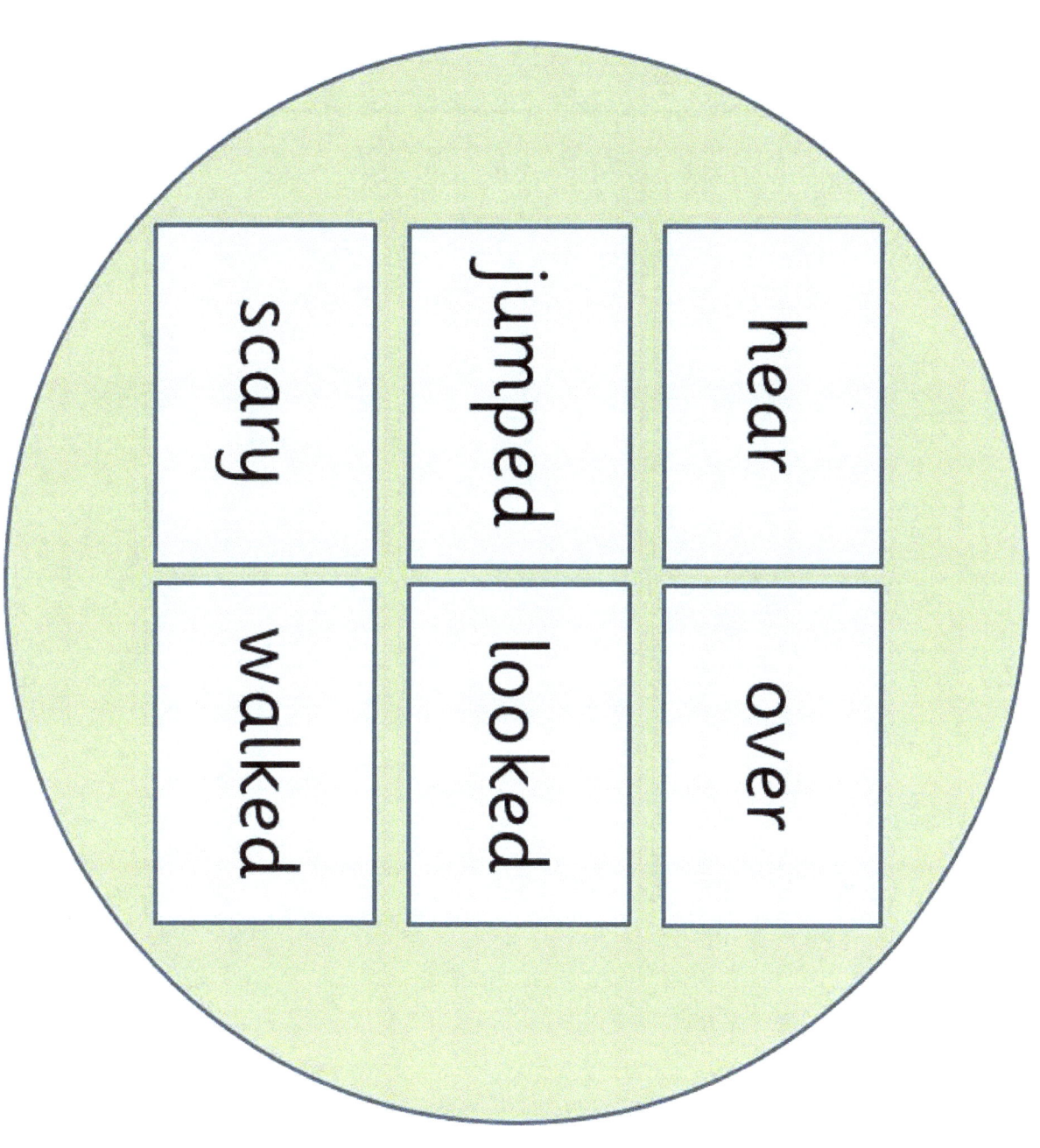

Book 15 Green board Spectro

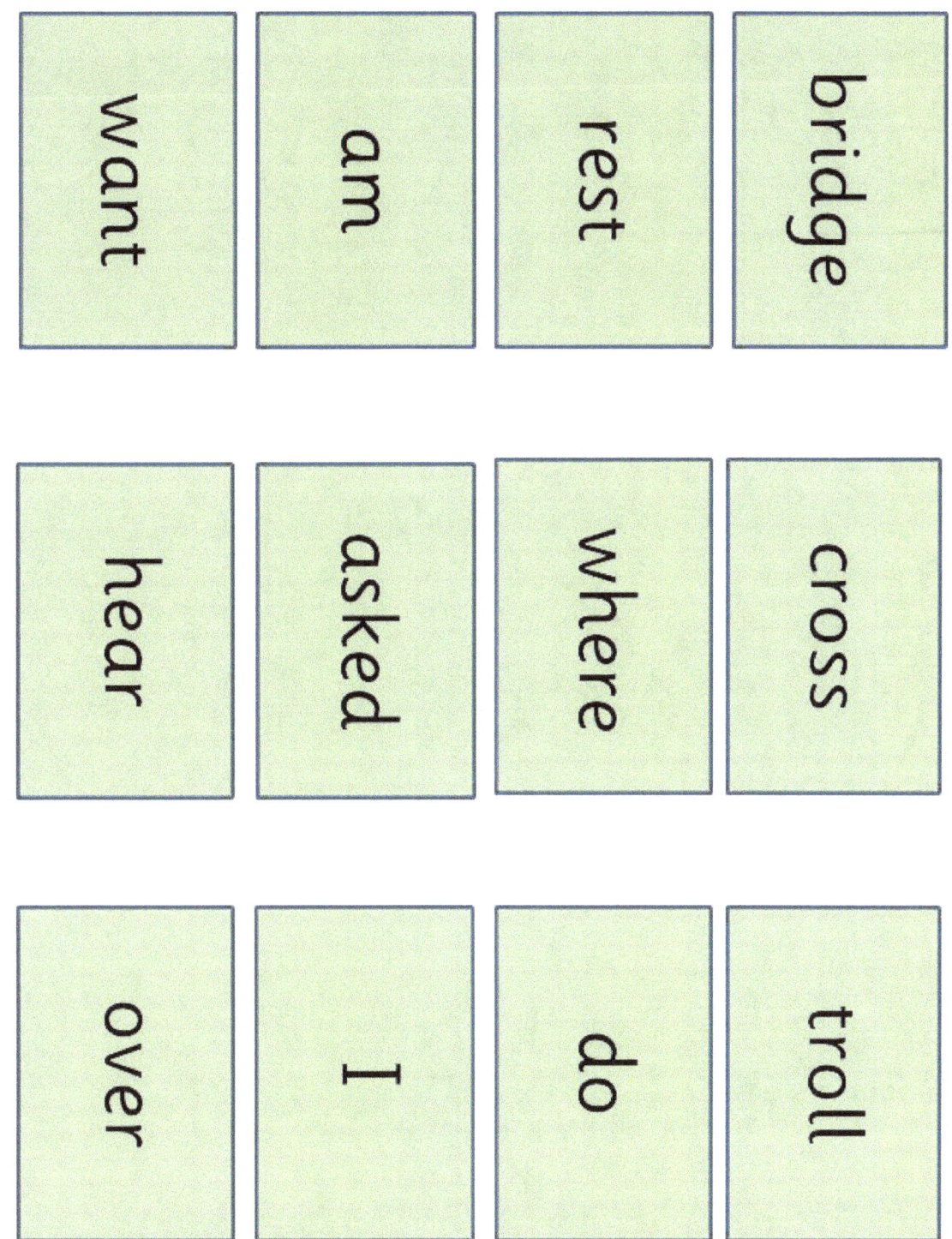

Book 15 Green words for Spectro. Words to be cut out and stacked on the circular board.

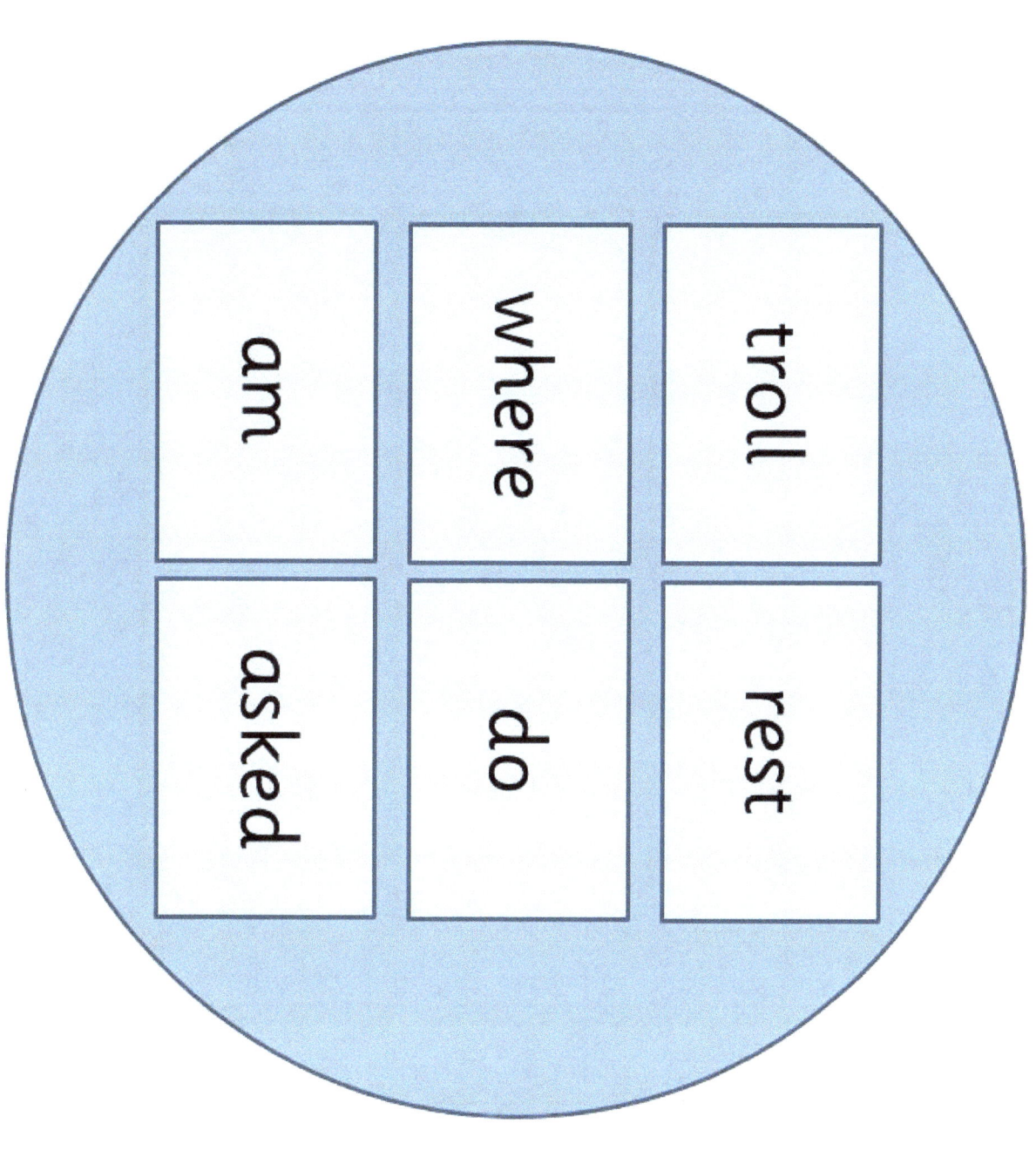

Book 15 Blue board Spectro

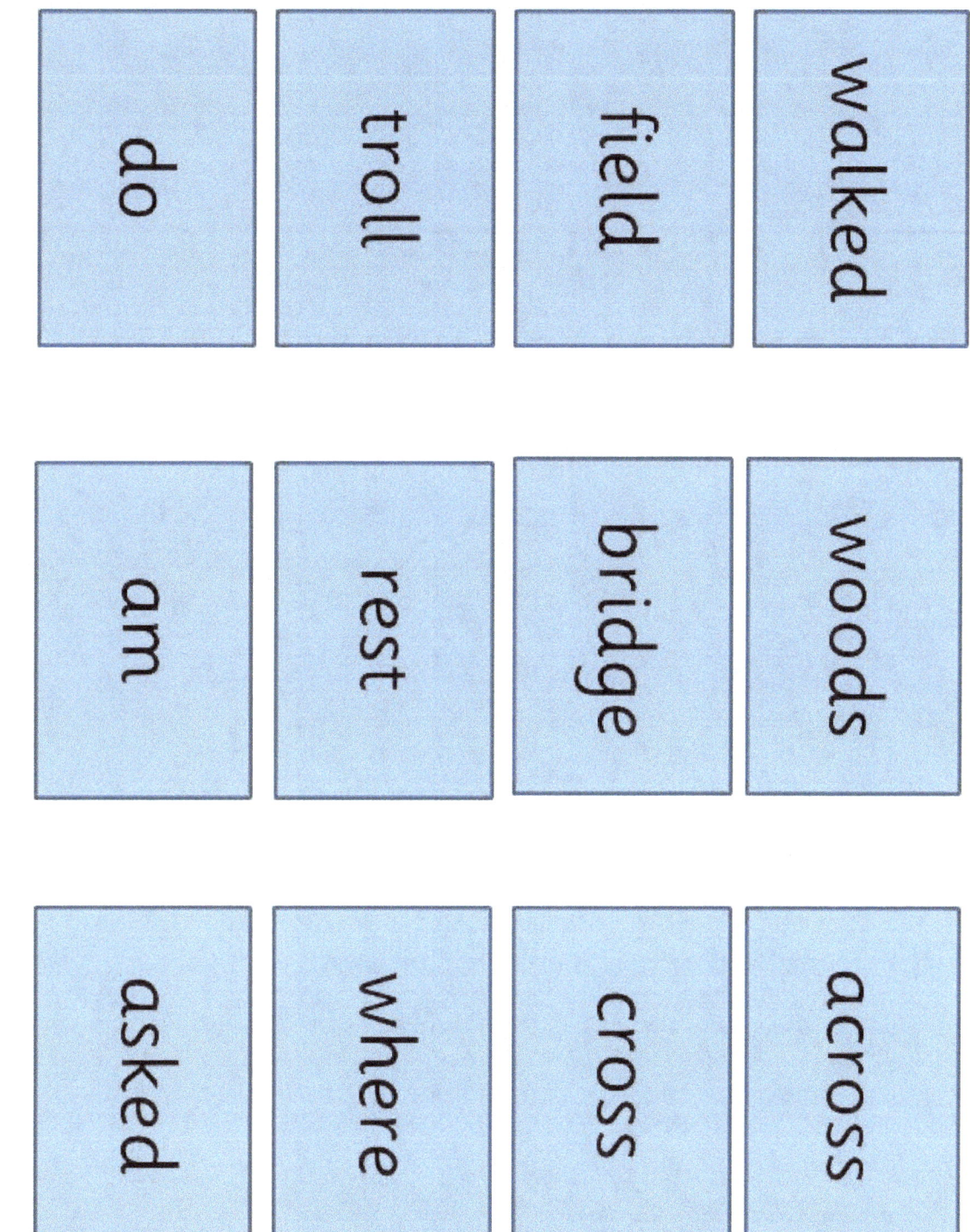

Book 15 Blue words for Spectro. Words to be cut out and stacked on the circular board.

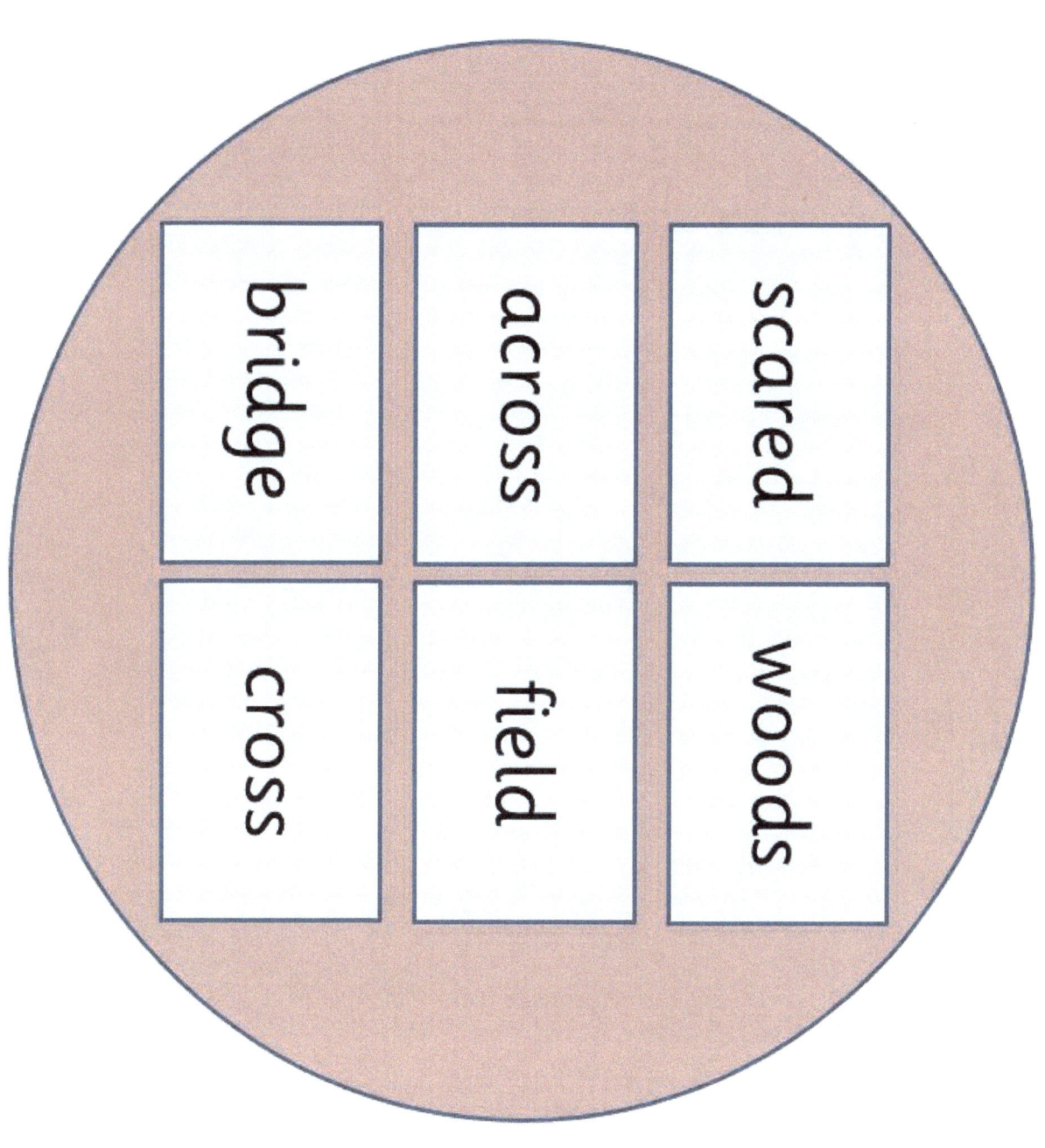

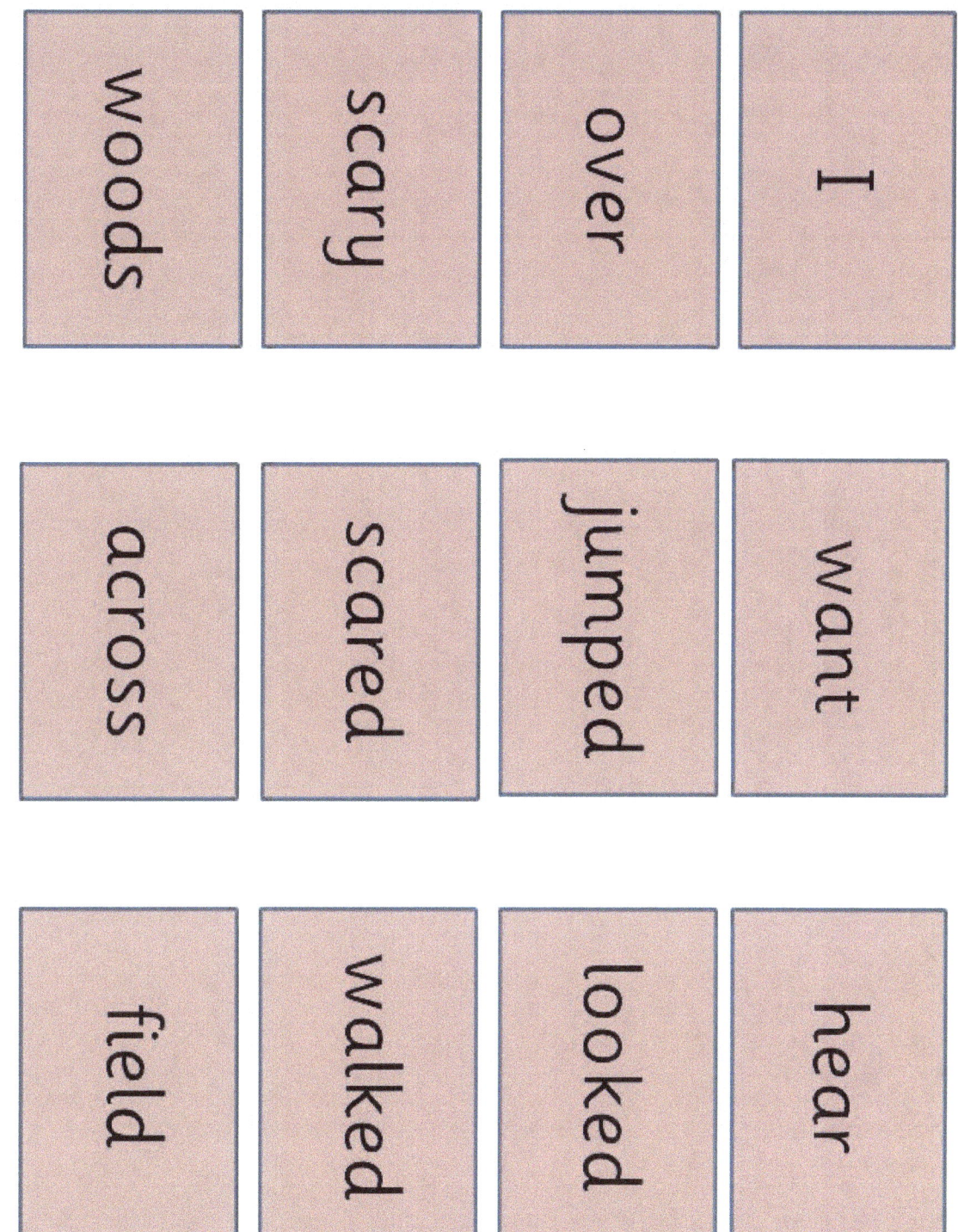

Book 15 Red words for Spectro. Words to be cut out and stacked on the circular board.

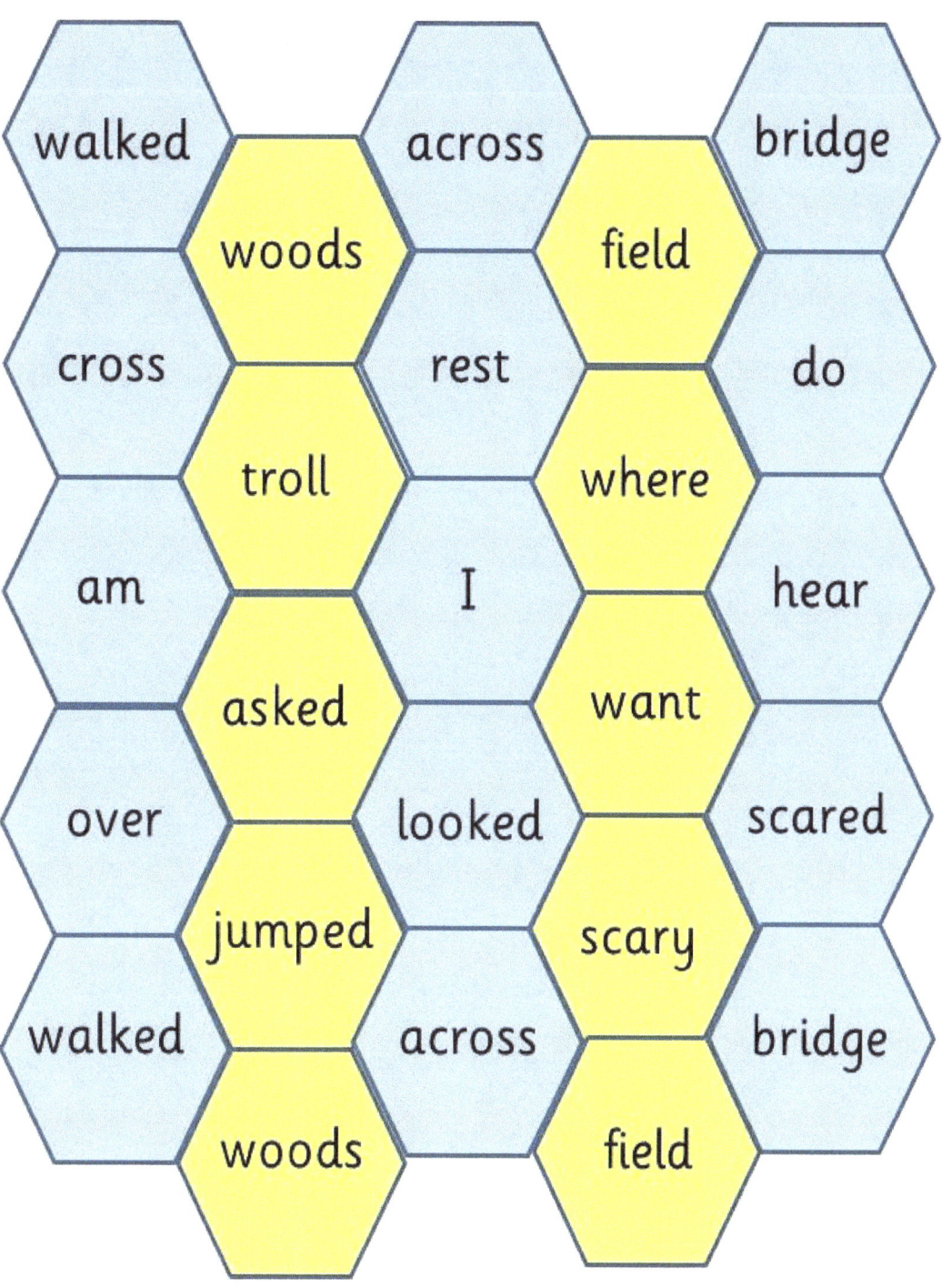

Book 15 Board 1 for Hex Connex

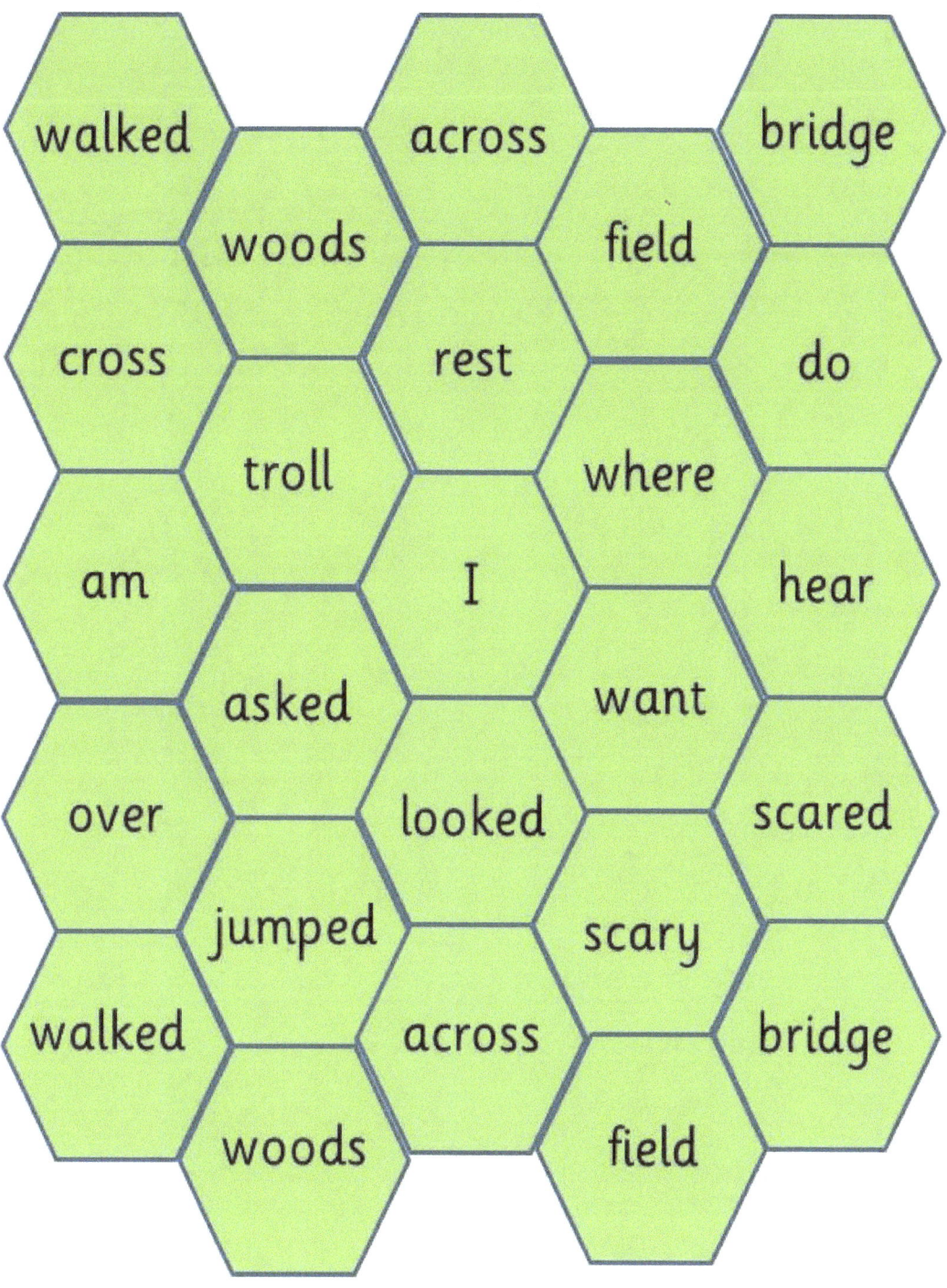

Book 15 Counters to be cut out individually for Hex Connex

Cut along bold lines and feed through the window

The butterfly 16

Word list:

wanted	crashed	work	flew	kept
make	foil	air	pointed	lifted
door	sure	or	don't	butterfly
could	if	boil	worry	only

Targeted phonics:
  st_
  _oi_
  _a_e

High frequency words:

work	make
door	if
or	don't
could	only

Text:
1. One day Zon wanted to make a door for his home.
2. Zon wanted a door for his shell. He went to the woods to see what he could find.
3. Zon went to where his metal ship had crashed. He looked for some foil to make his door. He got some foil from his ship.
4. Zon started to make the door. He was not sure if it would work. Flup came and asked Zon if he wanted some help. "You can lift the foil in the air," said Zon.
5. It was hot work. "I need some water or I will boil," said Zon.
6. Just then, Flup flew into the air. He pointed and said "Look, there is a scary monster in my home."
7. The old orange coat flew into the air. Zon was scared too. "What could it be?" he asked.
8. Flup and Zon went to find Grog. "We are sure there is a scary monster under the old orange coat," said Zon. "There is a monster in my home," said Flup.
9. "Don't worry," said Grog. "I am sure it is not a monster." They all went to have a look.
10. When they got back to the old wall, they could see the orange coat. The orange coat kept flying up into the air.
11. "We need to look under the old orange coat," said Grog. "You need to lift it up so that we can see," he told Flup.
12. Flup flew up into the air. He lifted up the old orange coat. They could see that it was a butterfly.
13. "Look, it is only a butterfly," said Flup. "Where is the caterpillar?" asked Zon. "It is a butterfly now," said Grog.
14. "I was sure it was not a monster. It was only a butterfly," said Grog.

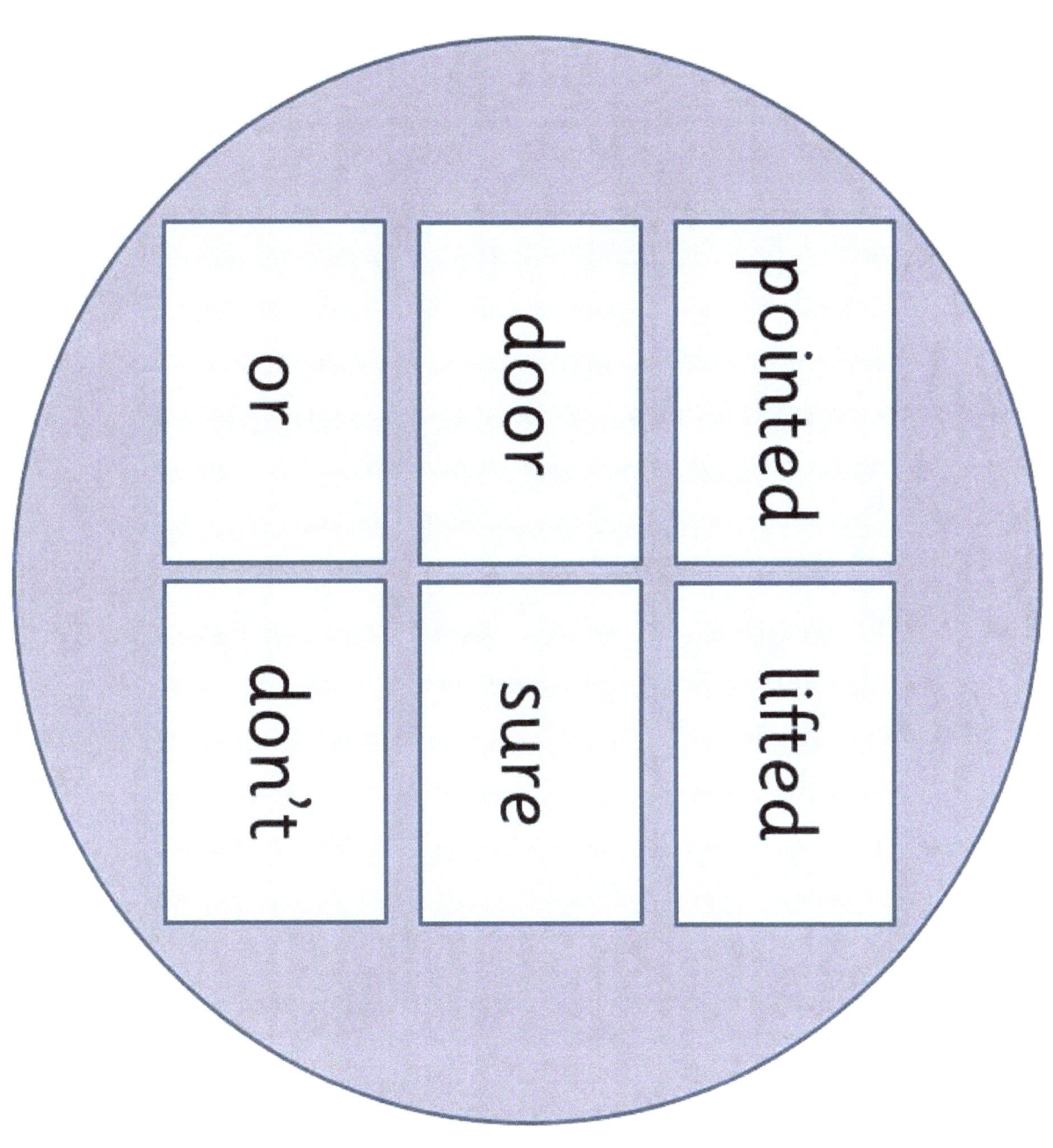

Book 16 Purple board Spectro

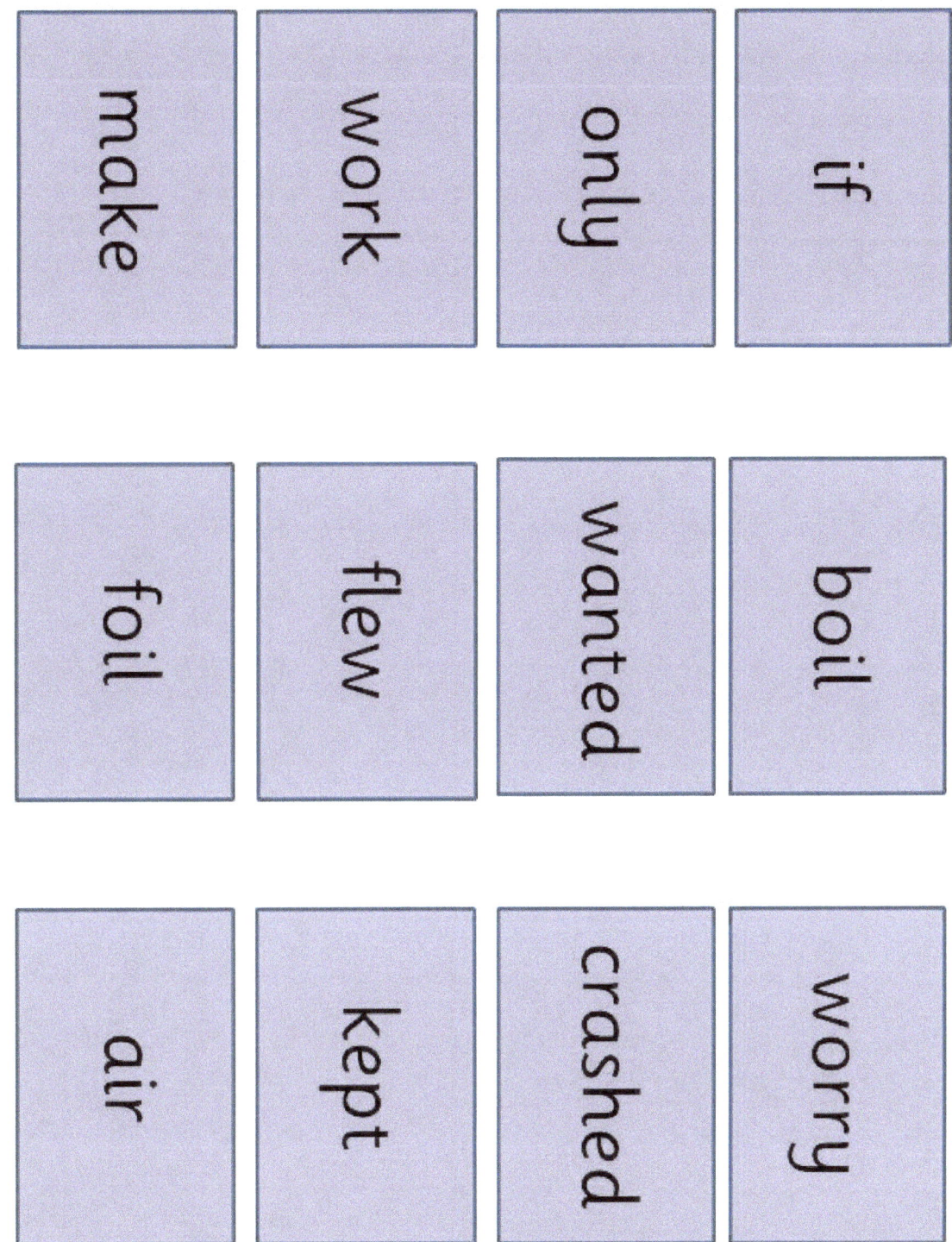

Book 16 Purple words for Spectro. Words to be cut out and stacked on the circular board.

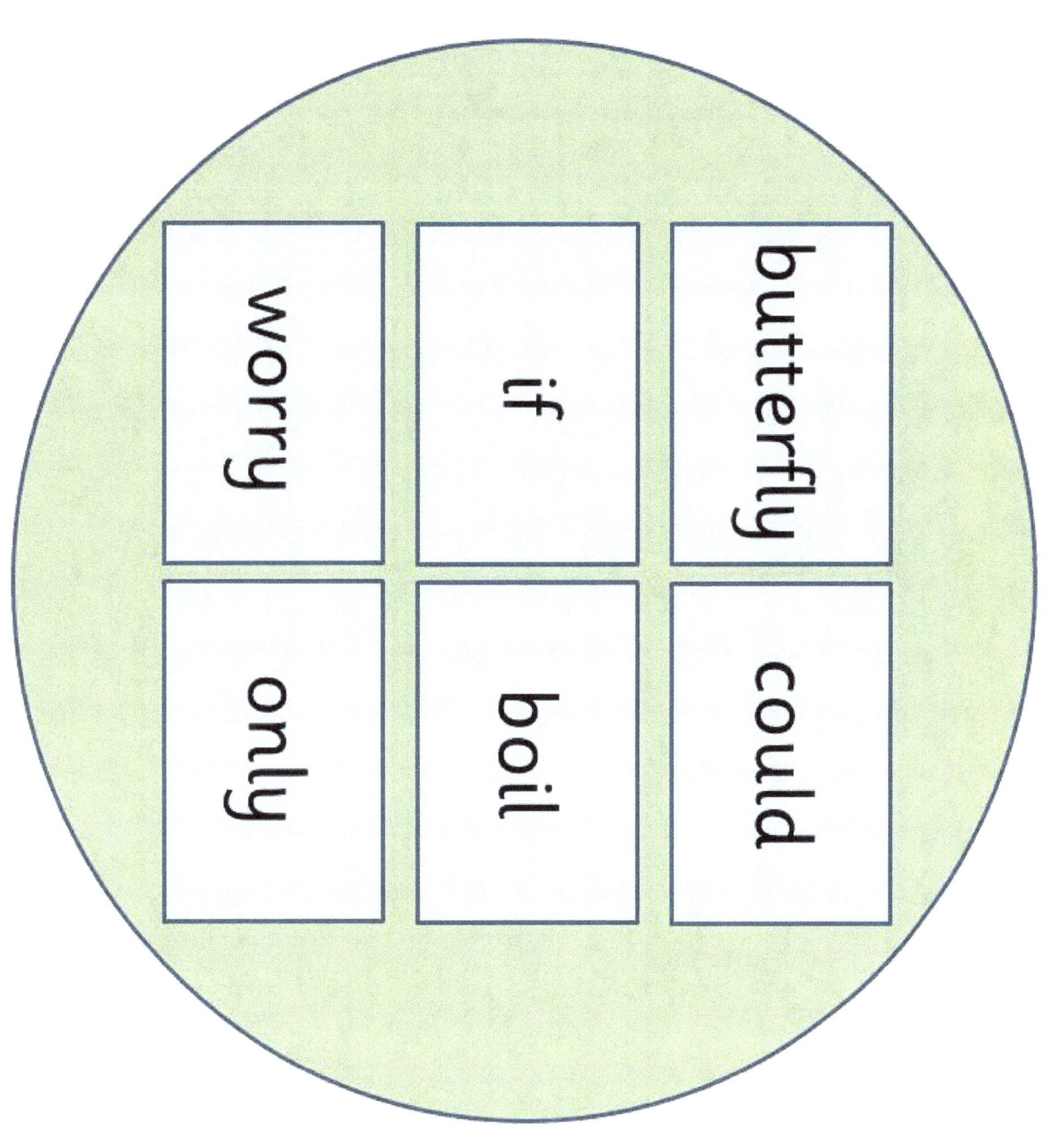

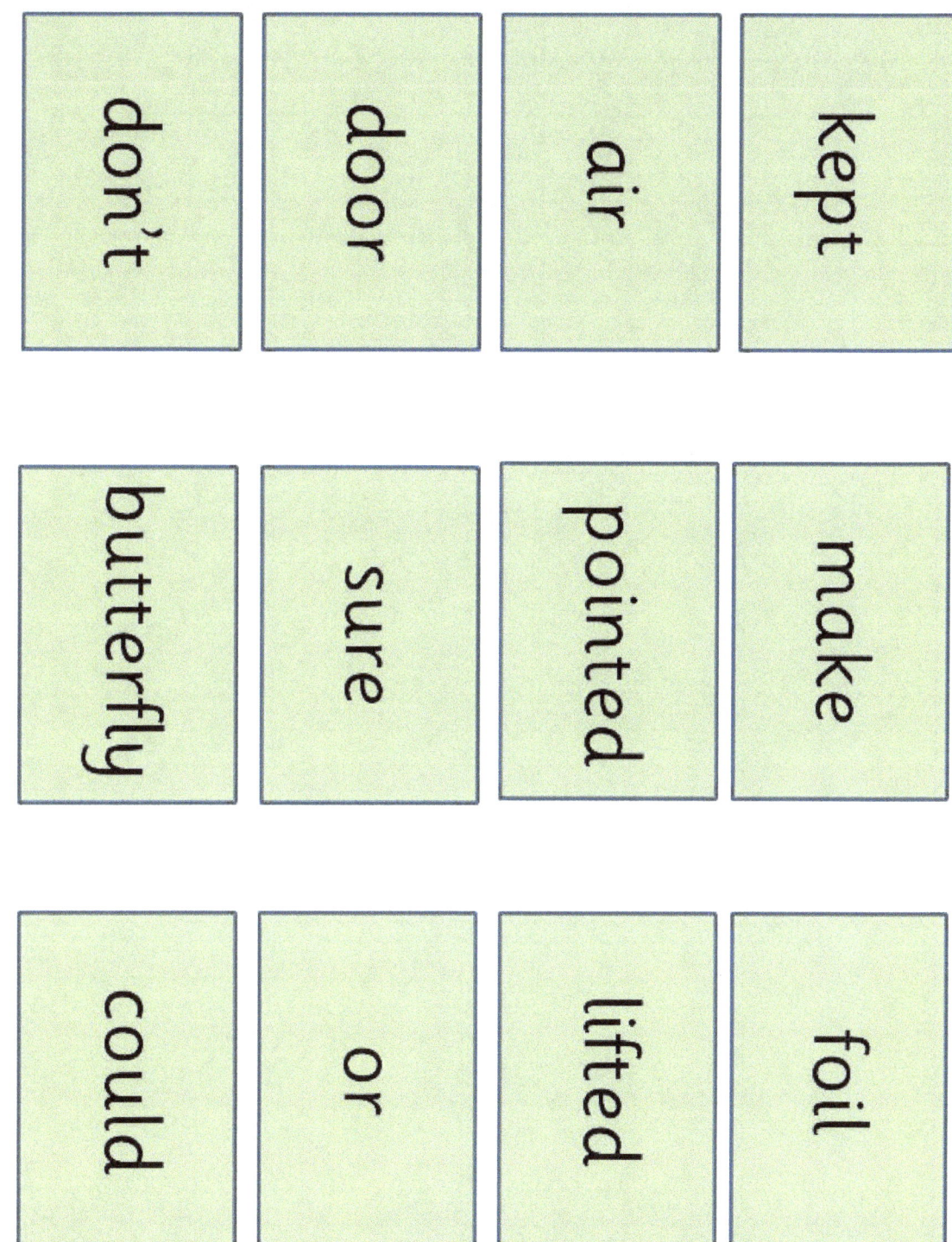

Book 16 Green words for Spectro. Words to be cut out and stacked on the circular board.

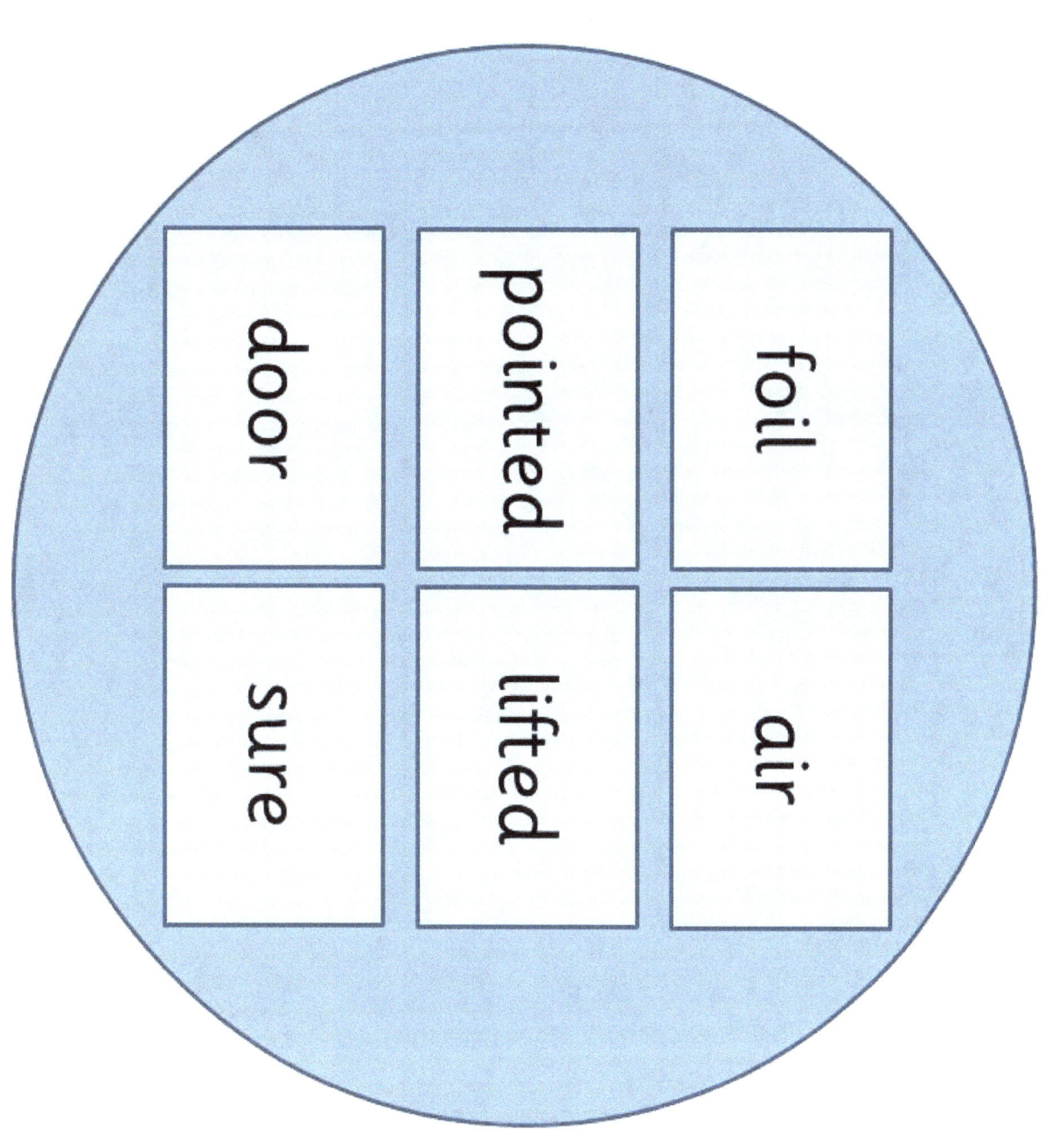

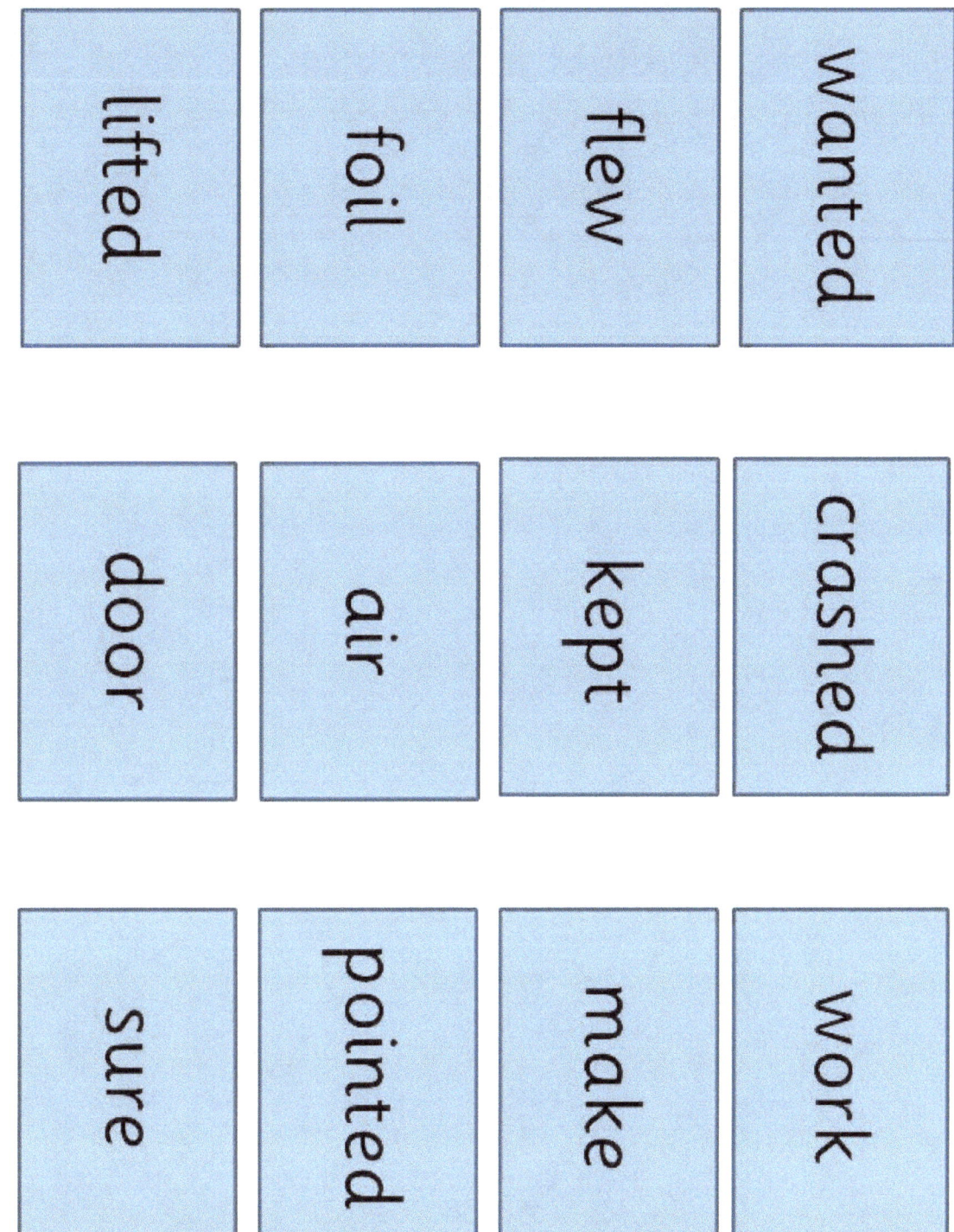

Book 16 Blue words for Spectro. Words to be cut out and stacked on the circular board.

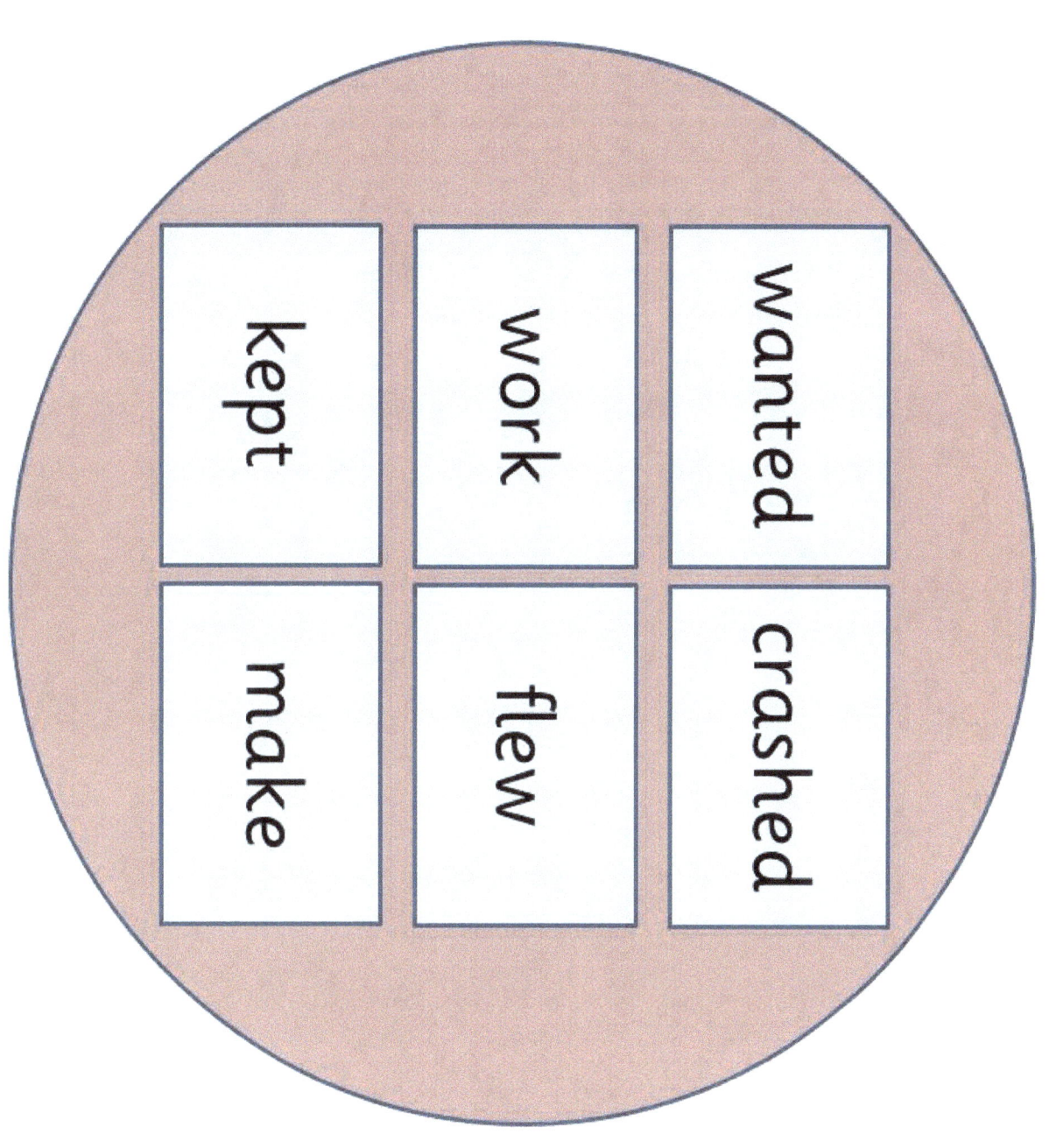

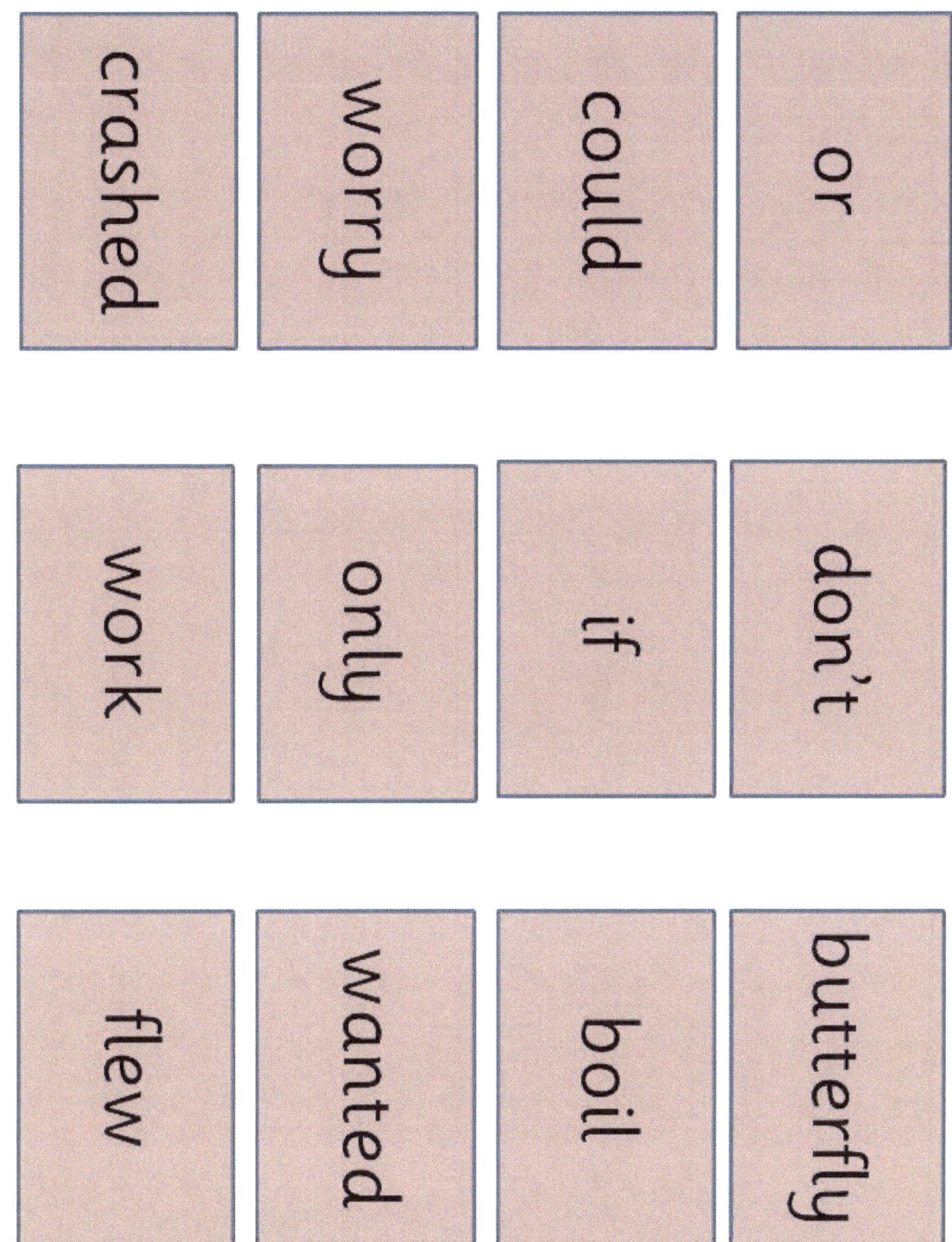

Book 16 Red words for Spectro. Words to be cut out and stacked on the circular board.

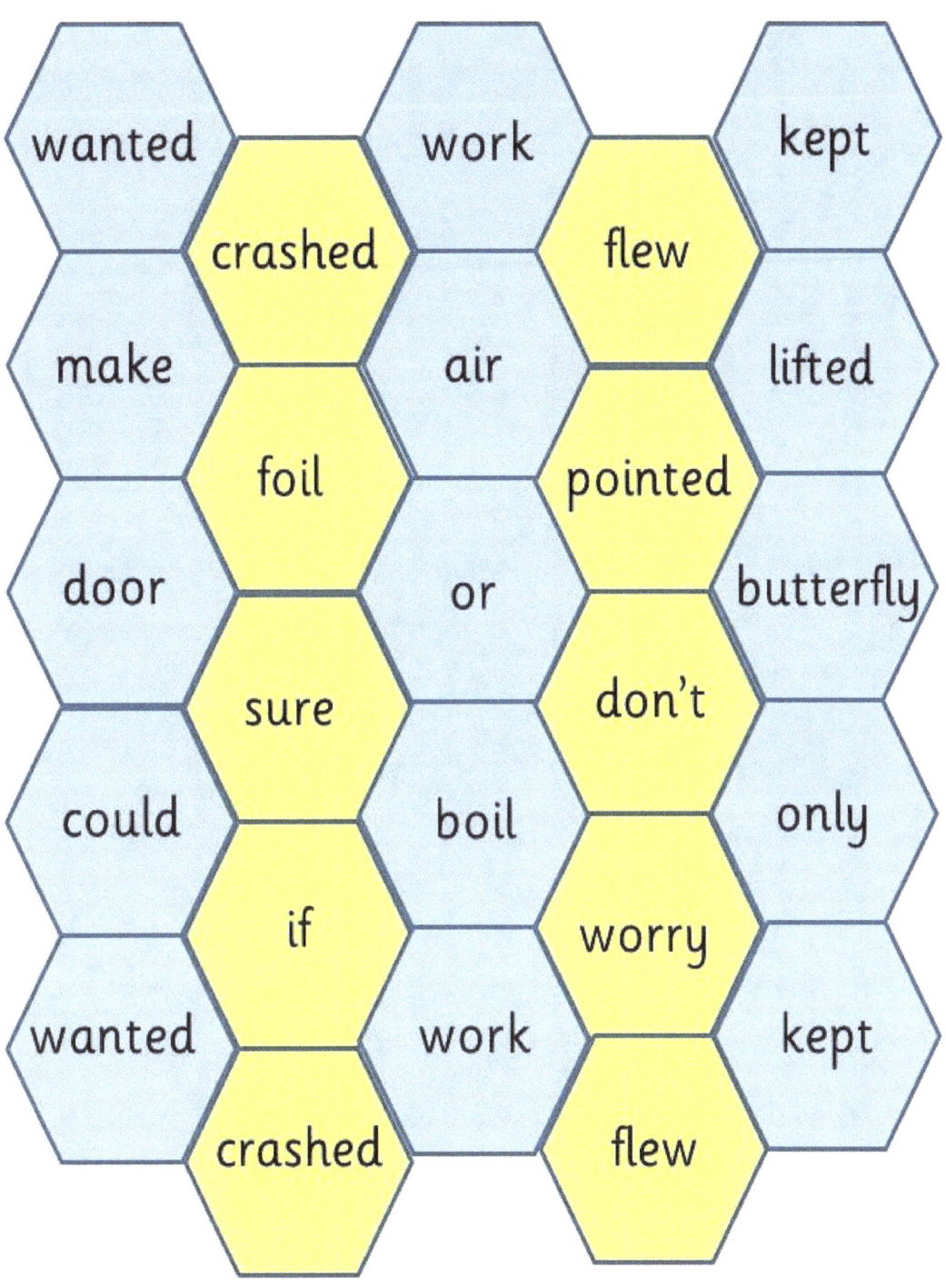

Book 16 Board 1 for Hex Connex

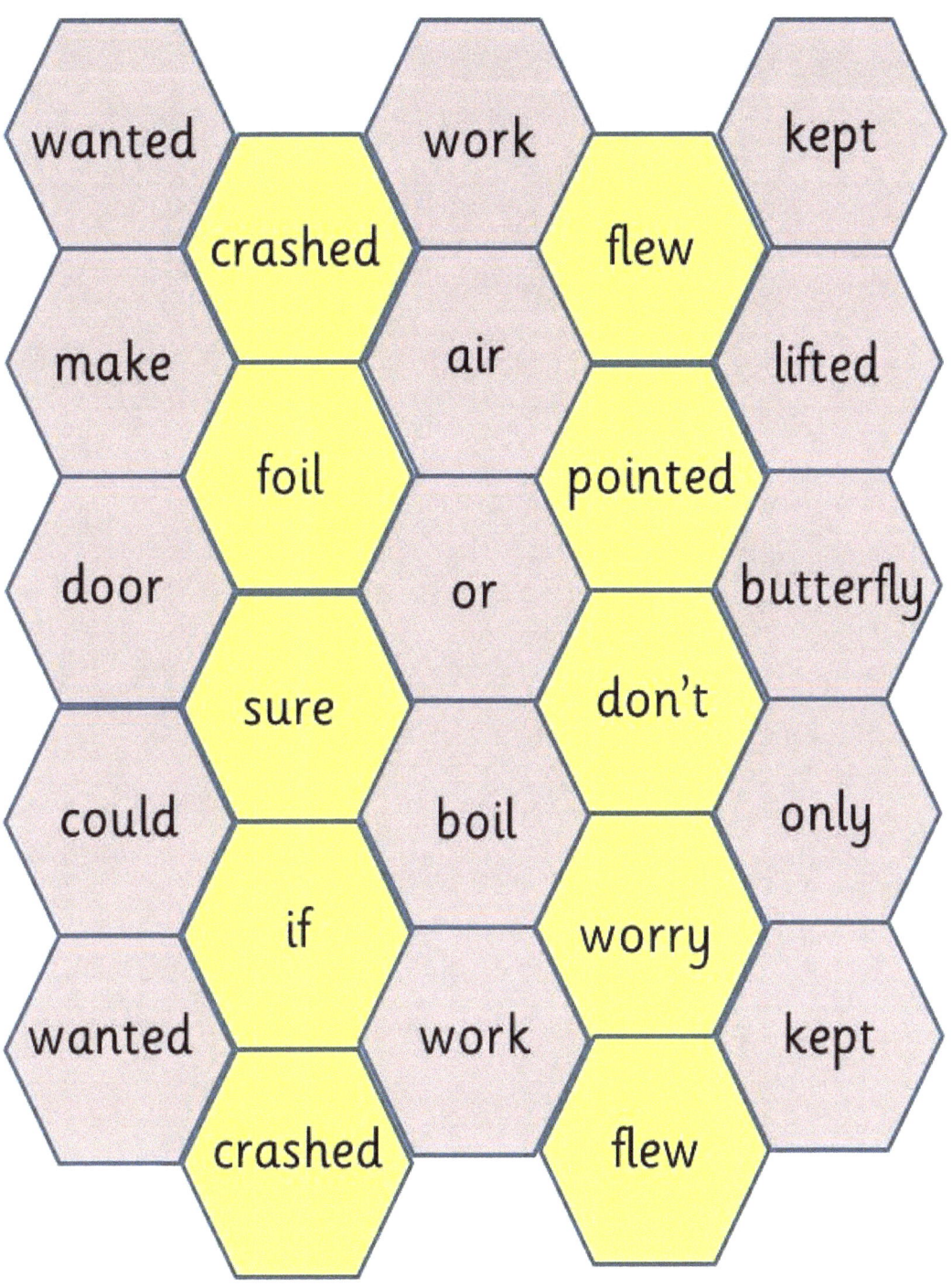

Book 16 Counters to be cut out individually for Hex Connex

Cut along bold lines and feed through the window

Pupil Tracker				
Name:				
Book	Activity	Date of 1st occurrence	Date of 2nd occurrence
9	Grog's Journey		
	Snakes and Ladders		
	Pento		
	Phonics sheet		
10	Grog's Journey		
	Snakes and Ladders		
	Pento		
	Phonics sheet		
11	Grog's Journey		
	Snakes and Ladders		
	Pento		
	Phonics sheet		
12	Grog's Journey		
	Snakes and Ladders		
	Pento		
	Phonics sheet		
13	Spectro		
	Hex Connex		
	Phonics sheet		
14	Spectro		
	Hex Connex		
	Phonics sheet		
15	Spectro		
	Hex Connex		
	Phonics sheet		
16	Spectro		
	Hex Connex		
	Phonics sheet		

www.ingramcontent.com/pod-product-compliance
Lightning Source LLC
Chambersburg PA
CBHW080430230426
43662CB00015B/2229